You Have Thre

Simply the clearest model

of the whole person

Volume ONE, Orientation

=:+:=:+:=:+:=:+:=:+:=:+:=:+:=:+:=:+

Bruce Dickson, MSS, MA

Tools That Heal Press

Resources by and for kinesiology testers
Best Practices in Energy Healing 100 level material
Composing your own vision of self-healing
The Nature of Human nature
Source code for the Psyche; Source code for Self-healing
Common language for personal-spiritual growing
All book descriptions at end of this book

HealingToolbox.org

CreateSpace ISBN 13 (4-28-12): 978-1475268775
CreateSpace ISBN 10 (4-28-12): 1475268777
Additional publisher inquiries welcome

eBook versions on Kindle, etc.

To Learn More:
http://healingcoach.org
http://HealingToolbox.org
http://selfhealing101.net
http://wholistic.theholisticchamberofcommerce.com

Dedication
Dedicated to John-Roger. Without you,
these resources would not exist.

Also to Bertrand Babinet, who
accelerated my understanding and
gave several of us
theoretical platforms and baselines
to build upon.

Tools That Heal Press

eBooks at Kindle etc.
HealingToolbox.org ~ *310-280-1176*
Longer *book descriptions at end of book*

- *Your Habit Body, An Owner's Manual* Our habits are our best friends; why then, do we make the same errors over and over again?

- *Self-Healing 101!* Best Practices in Healing System; How to Talk with Your Immune System, safety and permission to learn self-testing.

- *Meridian Metaphors,* Psychology of the Meridians and Major Organs

- "*Willingness to heal* is the pre-requisite for all healing"

- *You Have Three Selves Vol ONE*; Simply the clearest model of the whole person; Orientation

- *You Have Three Selves; Vol TWO* Simply the clearest model of the whole person, Find the 3S in your life & pop culture

- *The Inner Court*: Close-up of the Habit Body

- *The NEW Energy Anatomy*: Nine new views of human energy; No clairvoyance required

- *The Five Puberties,* Growing new eyes to see children afresh.

- *Radical Cell Wellness—Especially for women!* Cell psychology for everyone; A coherent theory of illness and wellness

- *How We Heal; and, Why do we get sick?* Including 35 better, more precise questions on wellness and healing, answered by a Medical Intuitive

- *You have FIVE bodies PACME*; Spiritual Geography 101

- **The Meaning of Illness is Now an Open Book,** Cross-referencing illness and issues
- **Rudolf Steiner's Fifth Gospel in Story Form** Topics include the TWO Jesus children and the active participation of the Buddha in the Christ event.

Gift eBooks:

Forgiveness, The Missing Manual

The Meaning of Illness Is Now an Open Book

The best solution is always loving
If you get stuck, give me a call.

To Learn More:
http://HealingToolbox.org
http://HealingCoach.org
http://wholistic.theholisticchamberofcommerce.com

Table of Contents

Many overlapping names for the basic self.......................7
The value of the three selves in four sentences...............12
Source code for the human psyche..............................13
The Kahuna connection...29
What is a "psyche" anyway?....................................30
Conscious self is the most isolated of the three selves......34
Many easy ways to grasp the Three Selves in your life......37
3S 101: The whole human psyche................................68
3S 102: Into the etheric......................................75
3S 103: Frequently Asked Questions...........................87
3S 104: A brief history of playfulness.......................89
3S 105: A few words on the psyche............................108
3S 106: The invisible is highly pattrerned & conditioned....98
3S 107: The largest pattern, Spiritual Geography...........151
3S 108: ENS-CNS dominance: Do you have
more thoughts or more feelings?................................167
3S 109: What each self does uniquely.......................197
3S 110: If we had NO helper selves.........................224
3S 111: Angels save us from boring art, music & poetry 232
3S 112: What was "The Plan" for human beings?..........239
3S 113: Source code for kinesiology testing.................246
3S 114: Any dangers in learning this material?............255
The Law of Gentleness
3S 115: Aligning with your own high self.....................260
Intimacy as into-me-see

Tools That Heal Press booklist descriptions...264

The future is already here;
it's just not very well distributed yet.
~ William Gibson, author, *Neuromancer*

Our willingness to heal
is only limited by our willingness to learn new things
about our own psyche

Many overlapping names for the basic self

The basic self is the operating system of the earthbound human psyche. It is the one who keeps all our conditioned bodies, cellular, imaginal, emotional, mental and mythological bodies, all coordinated. In computer lingo, this is the "shell program" enabling easy access to all capabilities from any other point in the system. Our operating system weaves all parts of our psyche together into a person who can both walk and chew gum at the same time.

How does it do this? This capacity to make a "web that has no weaver" is in the nature of the etheric body. The basic self is primarily an etheric being. Because our inner child is a subset of the larger etheric bodies of the Earth, solar system, etc, this is why it is relatively easy for information from these larger etheric fields versions to flow into our "silent partner."

Because it is the integrating factor and the operating system for the human psyche, the basic self has been "discovered" over and over again thru recent history and labeled with many names. All the following are functionally equal, from the conscious self point of view:

Some functional equivalences to "basic self" from the viewpoint of the rational intellect

- habit body
- animal self, animal nature
- Growth body, "etheric formative forces"
- immune system, the "floating brain"
- operating system of the body,
- neural default mode
- the body electric, life force,
- inner child, reactive emotional self
- memory body
- "feelings and needs" in the NVC sense
- the 'Little Artist' of *The Artist's Way*
- innate wisdom of the sum of your cells
- morphogenetic fields
- subconscious, unconscious
- gatekeeper of the etheric centers
- etheric body, etheric double

Q: WHY do you say these are all equal?

A: Several reasons. From the conscious self's point of view, you contact, communicate and negotiate with each of these in virtually identical ways:

acknowledgement, acceptance, curiosity, compassion, forgiveness; then, negotiate differences towards new behavior and resolution—just like you would with any child you loved.

Second, all and each of these have the wisdom of a three year old at least. This means they all understand the difference between what is "true for me now" and "not true for me now." K-testing does nothing more nor less than expand on and amplify this inherent wisdom.

Third, each of these can be communicated with via kinesiology testing-muscle testing-dowsing-inner testing —however you get a second opinion from your own internal sources. Further, the experience of communicating with each of these is so similar distinguishing between is virtually impossible.

The above names all overlap to such a high degree, differences between them are insignificant for most purposes. Distinctions between these can be made but are primarily of interest to clairvoyant sensitives and their researchers.

The most stringent test

of a *successful* psychology
has nothing to do
with adult ideas.
In fact, the most stringent test
of a successful psychology
has little to do with adults at all!

The excitement of personal-spiritual growth comes from discovering new potentials inside us, self-discovery as souls. Psychology has been regrouping around this simple idea since the 1970s.

To understand psychology, in my experience, has nothing to do with becoming a psychologist and little to do with reading or study. Rather to understand our psyche, you compose your own vision of the whole person.

YOU compose for YOU what "look and feel" is optimal for mental-emotional health. Yes, this is the "constructivist view" of education applied to psychology. Anything less is compost at best-- parroting what others have said at the worst.

Stumble into something revealing a wider view of the psyche, then we have something worthy of being called "psychology."

The most sane, useful, stringent, practical test, of any psychology is this:

Does it inspire young people to engage in personal-spiritual growth as lifelong pursuits--at the age when they are most receptive to this impulse?

More precisely, does the psychology in question encourage and inspire high school students, college freshmen and sophomores towards wellness?

Does it inspire young persons to engage with truly human values such as:

acceptance -> compassion -> understanding ->

forgiveness -> negotiation -> resolution

If a psychology inspires young adults to pursue wellness and truly human values—that's what we need.

I come at this topic in part from school teaching. K-12 schools are wonderful laboratories for observing developmental change because multiple age groups can be observed, in action, side by side.

Any school with multiple grades, in the realm of K-12, is a longitudinal "graph" of human development and maturation. If you have the eyes to see, the progression of age groups make healthy and unhealthy developmental change pretty obvious.

K-12 schools are natural places to field-test models of psychology that might encourage and inspire children to serve themselves, serve others, serve the world and grow for a lifetime—not just *consume* for a lifetime as too many conventional schools aspire to.

As far as I know, Rudolf Steiner's K-12 Waldorf school methods and curriculum model remains the closest anyone has come to a K-12 system likely to lead to appreciation of "I have three selves;" and, healthy balance between all three.

The value of the three selves in four sentences

1) The child who is well-cared for, becomes the adult who cares about them self, becomes a person who gives and receives easily.

2) The child who is unloved becomes the adult who has trouble caring for them self and trouble giving and receiving.

3) If guided sufficiently, children become adults with self-control, self-discipline, roots in the ground and wings to fly.

4) The child who lacks effective parenting as a child

remains childish even as an adult.

The 3S is source code for the human psyche

The three selves is open source psychology; anyone can play, learn and innovate.

So far the 3S paradigm has been mostly applied to healing and to personal growth issues; hence, the whole topic of healing the inner child.

The 3S can also be applied to muscle testing, kinesiology testing, dowsing, inner testing, or any other way of verifying and validating your own subjective impressions. This work began appearing in the very late 1980s and early 1990s in various convergences of Touch for Health and NLP, a topic taken up further elsewhere.

Computer open source software advocates like to say, "Transparency is the new objectivity." When too much information is the problem, simple transparency is highly valued. If the hologram of the human psyche is "too much info" for you, the 3S is a simplified view of the psyche highlighting the truly significant parts and making them transparently clear.

If there is another map-model of the hologram of the whole human psyche making It more clear than the 3S does, *please* contact me; I want to know. We will all gladly move on to that one.

What was wrong with 20th Century psychology and personality theory?

Well-read readers will know the 20th century had some ideas about psychology and personality theory. Several times in writing this volume I added and removed long sections comparing and contrasting the 3S with all the major humanistic 20th century psychologies. Currently this part is "out" because I see so little value in looking backwards. The surviving parts of this long compare-contrast conversation are the parts here and in volume two on Transactional Analysis, Gestalt and MBTI all of which are fully worthy to be carried forward into 21st century talk-therapy and holistic healing of all kinds.

Younger readers may not appreciate how mainstream psychology in the 18th thru 20th centuries, was the crippled step-child of medical pathology. The first 300 years of mainstream psychology was an offshoot of medical pathology, everything aimed at understanding mental-emotional-physical sickness, illness and deformity. The intent of pathology-focused psychology was to stop, label and fix illness. There was no "akido," no flowing with your opponent, no win-win solutions, only extermination of bad germs, bad feelings, bad behavior, and all undesirable traits. This created a 'mood of death' in mainstream medicine and psychology that prevailed until the early 1970s, when humanistic psychology, gestating since the end of WW II, burst into the mainstream culture and mass media.

The most explosive entry, among several, was Transactional Analysis (TA). TA offered dynamic, three-fold, moving, living representations of the psyche. However because TA did not address the spiritual capacity of human beings, it missed one-third of the human psyche. Over time it faded from view, superseded by more holistic approaches more open to the intuitive and spiritual capacities humans cherish.

To frame the question, "What was wrong with 20th century psychology and personality theory?" in a way it can be fairly responded to, given the new lights born in psychology from 1990 onwards, we have to reframe the question this way: "What was wrong with psychology and personality theory, founded on and focused on pathology and illness?" Most people reading this are inclined towards prevention and enhancing wellness than "looking backwards" to illness, pathology and dysfunction as proceeding as conventional medicine-science-psychology-medicine did from about 1750 to 1970.

Thinking on theories of personality circa 1971

Here's a telling snapshot from one page I saved from an unknown 1971 psychology 101 college textbook. It suggests the state of conventional wisdom about personality theory at the end of the 1960s:

> Personality theory is that portion of the psychological world given over to uncovering global principles describing

peoples' behavior. Personality theorists have the difficult job of explaining, in simple terms, everything anyone has ever done, can do, or might think of doing--even in the wildest of circumstances. A good theory of human personality must explain human sensations, perceptions, values, motivations, ability to learn and to change, how we relate to other people--and the theory must do so in terms fitting our understanding of our nervous system and the cultures we live in.

Psychology is still awaiting its Newton. But at least we have had our Freud, our Jung and Adler...while we wait for Newton to come along.

So then--pretty much as now in conventional mainstream thought--academics were looking forward to some Rosetta Stone, some clarifying and unifying principle or model to pull together and make coherent over one hundred years of observation in psychology.

Since 1971 conventional psychology has moved away from the medical pathology model, seeking only to know and address sickness; and, has attempted to move towards mental health enhancement, prevention and "positive psychology."

Still in conventional psychology no "big tent" in yet in view under which diverse psychological approaches-methods-protocols of personality theory find harmony. We want a unifying common ground, unifying denominators to permit useful observations from all insights to be pooled, towards more effective psychology.

A "big tent" for psychology won't be based on dysfunction, cannot start with what's deficient, broken and wanting in people. It must, begin with a vision of what is best in the human being, top to bottom, right and left, front and back. It must especially and explicitly embrace the spiritual and intuitive dimensions of human beings.

The separation of religion from objective science accomplished in the Age of Reason to the 1960s, has to be recalibrated to accommodate and be harmony with the rising frequency of the Earth.

After four decades of my own study, it appears the Three Selves is the best candidate for a unifying "big tent" in psychology.

Q: What about Brief Therapy, NLP, Positive Psychology and quick release therapies? Why aren't these stronger candidates for a "big tent"?

A: They could and they might become stronger. What would have to change is to rewrite psychology to incorporate the many capacities of being human that lie above the rational-sequential-logical mind.

At the moment, the Three Selves is the first, oldest and most coherent model of being human incorporating the many capacities of being human that lie above and beyond the rational-sequential-logical mind.

Briefly 19th and 20th academics and intellectuals tasked

themselves with ending the contamination of traditional churchianty thinking and politics into natural materialistic science. That was progress. For example, Rudolf Steiner was born in 1837. His parents were both "Free Thinkers." This meant they attended no traditional church services and accepted no inherited ritual dogma. This spirit of independent thinking was also prevalent in the Free Mason "founding fathers" of the American Revolution, seeking to "get a divorce" from the "group think" of church thinking and politics of the 1700s and earlier.

A hundred years and more later than Rudolf Steiner, psychology has moved so far away from anything intuitive, heartfelt or "spiritual" that the pendulum nows swings the other way. The smartest people actively seek to connect more strongly with their own Divinity in diverse ecumenical, exclectic and "free-thinking" appruaches.

The lack of any significant and effective conventional 20th century psychology meeting this need to encompass both concrete behaviors *and* human spirituality, created a void; and eventually a huge market filled by "New Age" and personal-spiritual growth literature.

Q: So why can't Brief Therapy be the big tent?

A: I guess the answer to that is partly above; Brief Therapy does not have--to my knowledge at least--an

EXPLICTIT acknowledgement of he spiritual capacities of people.

Politics play a role in this too. 20th century psychology was rarely "solution-oriented." Solution-oriented Brief Therapy" in the 1980s and cntinuing today, was therefore a big step forward. It continues to increase its intellectual "market share" since 2000 as evidenced by a continuing flurry of college textbooks. Brief Therapy builds on NLP in some connection I have yet to discern. And yet, Brief Therapy has been taken up only tepidly in the psychological establishment.

As Brief Therapy principles and practices have strengthened NLP practitioners who know of them; similarly, Brief Therapy principles and practices enliven the Three Selves for anyone who knows them. They are compatible. Any counseling approach that facilitates client movement towards understanding, empathy, forgiveness, negotiation and resolving win-win solutions is going to be compatible with the Three Selves.

Q: What about Martin Seligman's Positive Psychology?

A: The efforts of Seligman's *Positive Psychology* offer much to recommend. Unfortunately again, it fails to explicitly include, incorporate, identify and address human spiritual potentials above the mind.

I wish a living psychology of ALL aspects of the human

being had existed in the West earlier than the Thre Selves in 1948. God knows I have looked high and low in the literature.

Thanks to my mother, I cut my teeth, as they say, on Theosophy, Edgar Cayce, Yoga, Buddhism, Freud, Jung, Carl Rogers, Adler, and Fromm. I then spent another 15 years in Rudolf Steiner's Anthroposophy and Waldorf education, a tremendous catalyst to my growth. Yet even taken as a whole, their efforts didn't add up to much in this sense: each either avoided an explicit embrace of redirecting behavior in the habit body; or, human spiritual capacity, or both. They remained only partial models, from a holistic perspective.

Earlier drafts of this book had huge sections comparing and contrasting various 19th and 20th century models in light of the 3S, all gone now in this book. If you have a psychology that works for you--whatever it is--I celebrate that.

Energetic efforts were made to create a unified psychology in the 20th cntury especially after 1965. In today's terms the task was to outline a model to embrace both the entirety of our habit body; and, our spiritual potential, the "soul is choice" capacity we all have. I'm afraid a lot of heat but not much light was generated outside the Three Selves.

It may have been the rapidly rising frequency of the Earth that doomed many of the 20th century efforts to create a unified field theory in psychology. It may be as someone else said, a new explication of psychology is required every 20 years. So maybe something better than the 3S comes along pretty soon.

All that said, this articulation of the Three Selves could not exist without the contributions of Rudolf Steiner, Carl Rogers, Eric Berne, William Glasser, Touch for Health, and many others.

Marshall Rosenberg's Compassionate Communication, quixotically called Non-Violent Communication, is one of the very few psych modalities holding its own as a stable beacon of Light for psychological health and wellness next to the Three Selves and kinesiology testing.

Q: What about 100 quick-release modalities and therapies?

A: Since "NLP met K-testing" in the late 1980s, about 100 quick-release modalities and therapies have been developed by pioneering individuals. These include Immunics.org, Theta Healing, EFT and so on. More are surely coming. What does the 3S say about these new approaches?

This is another innovation conventional academic psychologists wish to ignore. Many people are getting results with these innovative health care modalities, at relatively low cost compared to psychiatry. A big tent of healthy psychology ought to encourage experiments and encourage integrity, ethics and standards. My study in these modalities over 40 years suggests the lens of the 3S provides clarity and insight into every one of the quick-release modalities. This book was written in part as theoretical support for all the new energetic and intuitive healing modalities and pioneers active since 1985. The 3S assists anyone to understand how and why these quick-release modalities work so well.

Is the 3S really a religion?

Thankfully, no. In all its history it's completely secular and ecumenical, applicable to all religion, one of the reasons its has spread so far so fast. In its Hawaiian embodiment, it has the most ritual; yet, even Hawaiian practitioners do not preach nor proselytize and prefer to remain somewhat hidden and obscure.

In the West the 3S really is no more nor less than an outline of the human psyche, in terms of health and how to work the psyche for the highest good.

This is a more living psychology than our great grandfathers passed down, the most living and most elegant model, so far found, to encompass all aspects of the psyche, for a psychology of health, hanging the frame from illness and pathology to health and wellness. Not more, not less.

A cooking lesson

Let's bake a cake. Take everything ever written about psychology. Subtract everything in the mood of pathology and death. Stop introducing high school and college students to psychology by way of corpse anatomy and illness.

Now add in everything positive ever learned about the human psyche. Connect all the dots that lead to health, wealth and happiness; loving, caring and sharing; abundance riches, and prosperity; and, touching to others with all of our goodness.

Now boil all that positive potential down into three and only three categories:

1) habits, behaviors and expressions here in 3D,

2) habits, behaviors and expressions connecting thoughts to feelings, feelings to thoughts and the art of observation, needs and requests,

3) unconditioned intuition and spiritual assistance in all its forms.

This gives you something like the three selves. That's our cake.

The 3S can be described as acknowledging the presence of every sort of human expression, with a direction towards reconnecting with your own capacities on each and all of these three levels, however you prefer to do that

Does the 3S simply repackage Eric Berne's TA?

Yes and no. I can find no evidence that Berne or TA practitioners knew about Max Freedom Long's three selves books and activity in the 1950s, according to library and online research. Yet, the two developed at the same time and had overlapping audiences.

The 3S since John-Roger tries to maintain the triumph of TA: reframing all of psychology and growth in a mood of playfulness. Psychology became a game anyone could play, no white lab coat was required any more. To talk about thoughts and feelings; anyone could do it. TA engaged young persons by making significant life learnings, game-like and fun. This was a huge step forward from the Freudian establishment, hard to imagine today.

Isn't the 3S just another self-help topic?

No. The 3S is about composing your own vision of yourself as a human being, from top to bottom, from how you connect with your own Divinity; all the way down to, how you acknowledge and redirect your own habit body. How these are IN YOU becomes YOUR own positive psychology for the purposes of YOUR growth.

Q: Hmm, that could be really useful for my personal goals.

A: Yes.

Q: It could be really useful in K-12 education.

A: Yup.

Q: It could be useful for counseling, psychotherapy, any talk-therapy. Then those smart people could argue less and cooperate more.

A: Yes. If there was ever a broad consensus within twentieth century psychologists, that embraced human intuitive and spiritual capacities, I cannot find it. Most 20th century specialties were in heavy intellectual competition with each other about the nature of the human being in all aspects except spiritual things. There is so much good work in the past 120 years of understanding human growth. So far as I know, no paradigm has been big enuf to integrate it all, to bring it all together; until now. You can decide if that's true for you.

How to get the most out of this book

Whoever has the most fun reading this book, wins

This is the most fun book I was able to write. As John Morton of MSIA says, relaxation and fun are the best ways for us to learn. See a way to make this more fun? Tell me. This is the first attempt ever at a comprehensive textbook on the three selves. I don't know everything; I don't even wish to. I fully expect readers to suggest massive improvements by phone, email, Pony Express, etc.

One way I had fun composing these two volumes was using each topic to open a new door in my own psyche. If the door lead to a new space uncomfortable to me, I went in anyway knowing--as long as it's safe—when the unfamiliar becomes familiar, it becomes comfortable.

See what kind of journey you can take.

How to discuss new ideas that are both above and below the mind

No one in their right mind would attempt writing a book outlining everything known on the three selves. But you don't have to be in your right mind to read this book.

Wait--that didn't come out right. How about this: if you are on a path of personal and/or spiritual growing, staying curious and open is crucial. We are all looking for the lost pieces of our own potential. To re-claim them, peeking around the obstacles in your own psyche and stepping outside your own "box" is required over and over.

For me, this book was part of my journey, a kind of *Becoming Fully Human For the Complete Idiot*. The very relaxed "voice" developed here deliberately contrasts with the formal style of psychoanalytic writings and APA style. In the formal style, the goal is to get things right. The goal here is to engage you to consider the larger field of your entire psyche, two-thirds of which is outside your rational mind, your waking conscious self. If I can arrange things so you feel safe to explore and have permission to explore your own lower basement and upper attic, I will have done my job.

This is a book of open secrets. They simply aren't widely known–yet. If ideas here appear mysterious, be gentle with yourself. No one assimilates a lot of new ideas quickly.

If you find yourself frustrated with the non-linear nature of this book's organization, come back to these front sections. Find a diagram or characterization you relate to, find a connection with your own personal life. Build from there.

What's the dif between Vol. 1 & Vol. 2?

Vol. 1 gives you the source code to learn about and operate your own psyche. The 3S is the nature of human nature, in the 3D experience, incorporating how to connect with your own Divinity.

Vol. 2 points out where the 3S are visible around you:

- in the human body,

- in the landscape of popular media.

It also builds bridges to Transactional Analysis and other psych models whose use is enhanced and expanded when viewed thru the lens of the 3S model.

If all you take away from this book is ideas, that's unfortunate

Go for experience. As they say: if you meet the Buddha on the road, gobble him up, assimilate him entirely and keep moving forward towards higher ground.

Feel free to start anywhere and read anywhere. If you get confused, go back a chapter or more. Skip any chapter that doesn't work for you. Come back to it later.

This volume is not everything about the three selves. Find many signposts where to go to learn more. If you find ideas that should have been included, contact me.

Additional good sources on the three selves

- *Your Inner Child of the Past*, Hugh Missildine, M.D. The first book and classic on the inner child I believe. Surprisingly, this remains perhaps the BEST book on the inner child. Written by a child psychiatrist with great exposure to the patterns of dysfunction in childhood, Missildine spells out patterns you can recognize in yourself and others. Later inner child books, except

Bradshaw, often lack this breath of vision.

- Psychotherapeutic books written since about 1985, on pretty much any topic.

- Concise books on Huna/Kahunas. Tow more accessible summaries known to me are Sondra Ray's *Pele's Wish* (Inner Ocean, 2005) and Max Freedom Long's *Secret Science at Work* (DeVorss).

- Margaret Paul's *Inner Bonding* books and website.

The Kahuna connection

The three selves model entered the West thru Max Freedom Long's series of twenty-odd books for DeVorss, starting in 1951. Traditional practitioners of Huna are called Kahunas. Blessings on all kahunas everywhere! Much has been written on the kahunas; however, in the shamanic tradition of Hawaii, the intricacies huna require learning the Hawaiian language literally and in detail.

This linguistic approach to personal-spiritual growth has taken hold in the West only very feebly despite 50 years of effort. Kahuna wisdom transposed to the language of counseling and psychotherapy, especially since 1985, is what Westerners find more accessible and this book continues in that vein.

cCcCc

What is a "psyche" anyway?

Here's how we're going to define "psyche," since it's defined variously.

Psyche is the sum of one individual human consciousness in 3D incarnation.

The psyche is everything in the thinking mind, everything in the feeling mind,

everything in the sub-conscious and

everything in the unconscious.

This means psyche includes everything you know about yourself and everything you don't know about yourself but which is still present within you—somewhere, everything present in you, known and unknown. That's the psyche, your psyche.

We will use the word "personality" as a near synonym for "psyche." To me, you are what you are, whether you know all your facets consciously or not. This truth is especially evident in a client practice. How clients self-identify is often a mere fraction of what a neutral observer sees presented. This is one reason why we need each other to heal; we are each more transparent to others than we are to ourselves.

Why the 3S is so difficult to write about

Unlike mainstream psychology of the 18th to 20th centuries, the 3S is about the entire psyche. Psychology of the 18th to 20th centuries started and ended, more or less, with the rational mind, explaining other aspects and aberrations of the psyche in rational terms.

The 3S does not assume the pshche begins and ends, lives an dies, on the point of view of the rational mind because this is the part of us most like an isolated island, most like the famous cartoon of a single man existing meagerly on a tiny desert island in the middle of an ocean.

Rather the three selves takes a different perspective; namely, our isolated "man on an island" self wants to, needs to, must learn about the other two-thirds of his own psyche. This is the only way for him to expand his possibilities from the single tiny island (of rationality) he lives on.

However because a full one-third of our psyche is *above* our rational mind; and, another full one-third is *below* our rational mind, it's challenging to write about three-thirds of the psyche and make sense to the little one-third!

Add to this task the little one-third-self reading this book has very little or no language for its other two-thirds, unless it already knows Ho'oponopono or has done extensive inner child work, both still a rarity.

On top of that, most everything we are going to discuss is invisible; worse, 90% of what makes us truly human is also invisible; only our bodies are perceptible and "real" to "hard science;" everything else is "unreal" or vague or very variously defined by hard science.

Anybody can jot down the bare bones system of the 3S; many books do just that in one or two pages. But grasping the *system* of the 3S is not the *experience* of your basic self, not the *experience* of your high self. Some readers will know Transactional Analysis foundered on this same shore, trying to make the system real enuf to experience when all along it's obvious you only experience the topic when you drop and let go of the system, let go of how you think about your self and experience your self.

Updating the psyche into contemporary language, needs doing every generation, every 20 years, someone said. I think this is correct these last 150 years. To learn the 3S requires living your way thru it, living into your own three selves. It takes a while to do that, even using the 3S as a guide. All the ideas and uncoveries here have held up for my own personal use for two years to 30 years. I can't think of anything in this book that has yet to pass that test. See if any of it works for you.

.vVv.

Communication between selves

At each of these three levels, the selves communicate with each other. Conscious selves access each other primarily by talking. Basic selves access each other primarily by body language, frequency and empathy.

Both basic and high selves communicate on many other non-verbal levels both above and below the preferred communication channels of the rational mind. Your individual b/s and h/s are always in touch.

Whenever two or more people meet, all selves involved connect as deeply as the two conscious selves "negotiate" to connect. The c/s is often completely unaware in the moment of what connection their lower and higher selves are making with the other person's lower and higher selves. You can get in on this conversation, but it takes practice.

The best place to start expanding your communication is to acknowledge, accept and communicate with your own basic self. This takes curiosity, commitment and practice to do well and easily.

Talking with your basic self is similar to talking with children. Imagine talking with a three year old child even if your basic self's developmental age is older. Somehow a child "three years old" is what prompts the c/s to remember it must modify how it speaks with a child. It must speak with love, caring and authenticity if it wants the attention of the child. That's the secret. If you practice, you will get better.

Communication between the c/s and the high self takes place automatically as a beneficial side effect of open, loving communication between conscious and basic self.

The conscious self is the most isolated

of the three selves

By design the c/s is the most isolated of the three selves. The c/s is "out of the loop" of the basic and high self (John-Roger).

To paraphrase Rudolf Steiner, if the soul had to do all the jobs here, breathe the air, pump the blood, digest the food—it would have very little time to evaluate all our options in all our choices and decisions. This is why the rational mind is so isolated, to free it up from distractions, so it can focus on its main job of exercising healthy choices and making better decisions.

So the conscious self is isolated by design, giving it freedom to practice making healthier choices; as Socrates put it, to do the right thing, at the right time, with the right person, for the right reasons.

Soul is choice. The angels are working overtime to preserve for us our ability to choose.

To switch metaphors, the b/s and h/s are cut from the same cloth; the c/s is cut from different cloth.

This helps explain why the low self and high self have been cultural blind spots in mainstream psychology. When the rational mind begins looking for other selves like itself, other intelligence near at hand, and acknowledging it is NOT alone, then it finds its closest and best friends. One is slightly lower lower in frequency; one is slightly higher in frequency.

NLP: The c/s has a preferred,

most open channel of communication

NLP uncovered how the conscious self prefers to receive information thru visual, auditory, kinesthetic-feeling, smell-taste, percepts. The ration mind prefers one of these percept channels over the other channels.

The basic self also has a preferred,

most open channel of communication

The Three Selves extends the right to have a preference for perceptual input, a most open channel of perception, to the basic self, to our gut brain.

The basic self prefers and will attend to first, percepts coming in thru its most open, preferred channel of communication. It will be: visual, auditory, kinesthetic-feeling, smell-taste.

Whichever communication channel is most open in the basic self, that will be the easiest channel on which to "talk" with your inner child.

C/s and b/s have different preferred

most open communication channels

The c/s and b/s are often have different favorite perceptual channels. The basic self's channel is typically one "down" in frequency from the channel the c/s prefers. If the c/s is predominantly visual, the b/s is likely to be predominantly auditory or kinesthetic.

Find your basic self's most open communication channel(s) and you have the biggest key to developing a common language between c/s and b/s.

Your b/s's most open channel of communication is where you will be able to "hear" your immune system responding "true for me now" and "not true for me now."

K-testing is a good way for selves to communicate

Several effective techniques exist for the c/s to bridge gaps between it and the basic self so communication can resume:

- Gestalt Therapy, empty chair technique
- Voice Dialogue
- University of Santa Monica, Self Counseling
- kinesiology testing and self-muscle testing
- Compassionate (nonviolent) Communication

All of these are good ways for the c/s to communicate with the b/s. These are primary techniques in the most effective inner child work.

See 3S 113: 3S is source code for kinesiology & muscle testing for more.

v\V/v

Many easy ways to grasp

the Three Selves in your life

Why so many metaphors, definitions, angles? Recursiveness

The thesis of this book is "you have three selves." Making my case for this is challenging because to do so, I have to make yu curious about things above your mind; specifically, your nature as an etheric being.

The Theosophists tried for most of 100 years to explain the etheric body in mental, logical sequential terms. You can see their efforts in books like The Etheric Double: *The Health Aura of Man (Theosophical Classics Series) by Arthur E. Powell*. Few people read these books now and virtually no young persons at all. The intellectual-scientific approach to the etheric body was a spectacular failure as an educational approach. The virtually fruitless endeavor to make the etheric body mind-friendly continues in books like *The Field* by Lynn McTaggert despite the author's very considerable appeal as an author.

The three selves cannot be discussed effectively in conventional term paper structure: introduction, thesis (up to three), explication and conclusion. Linear, sequential, logical APA format is wonderful exercise for developing intellects and appropriate for topics where we wish to learn the logic and working of things--up to and including mind topics.

For things with origins above the mind, you have to give up that approach. Mental topics, logic, all call for CLOSURE. Etheric topics call for being OPEN.

The widespread popularity of Rumi's idea of, "There is a field beyond right and wrong; I'll meet you there" comes from today's yearning to go eyond and above he mind, beyond what can be accomplished by closure alone.

Above the mind, to grasp the human psyche, requires poetry. Want to see more than the mind alone can see? You have to relax on the linear intellect and "stretch" to embrace the *whole*, not the *parts*.

The merely rational mind cannot grasp a hologram because there is no one way to understand it. A hologram is all parts connected to all other parts and ability to get from any one part to any other part directly; hence, the useful idea of a hologram as a community of related points and resources.

Where intellect fails us, intelligence takes over.

The human psyche is only restricted to logic from the mind down. Above the mind, in your upper etheric body and your mythological frequency, logic does not bind you; tho, faulty archetypes may.

To make the case "you are an etheric being" requires getting readers off-balance enuf that they will reach for support to steady themselves; and then, offer them support above the mind.

Some readers will know we use "Closed" and "Open" here exactly the way they are used in Meyers-Briggs Type Indicator (MBTI). Closed and open-spontaneous are termed called Judging (prefers Closure) and Perceiving (prefers sPontaneity) in that system; for example, "Goodbye" connotes 'closure' (J). "Aloha" connotes 'beauty forever' (P). See a more complete discussion of MBTI in *The Inner Court.*

Our multi-faceted human psyche can only be gestalted, not spelled out. Because each person learns uniquely and learning styles are not only multiple but infinitely varied, it helps to approach understanding of the 3S in multiple ways, in recursive spirals of meaning, new layers of meaning overlaying earlier understandings. Be prepared to see the same topic covered several times from different views here, a good thing.

Poetry is what we use to discuss topics above the mind. Please consider the following multiple summaries and metaphors for the 3S as different facets of the same diamond. Take and use the ones that ring your bell; leave the rest for others coming up behind you.

The over-and-over nature of the 3S discussion makes this writer vulnerable to accusations of sloppy writing. Recursiveness is no excuse for poor writing. If readers see better ways to layer in meaning than I have done here, let me know. I'll take all the help I can get!

The basic self as "habit body"

More commonly known as the "inner child," the basic self is even more usefully termed the *habit body*. That's the one breathing us right now. We don't actually breathe consciously. The conscious self only occasionally attends to the rhythms of breathing. We *can* breathe consciously; but frankly, the conscious self has more pressing and interesting things to do.

What does the basic self want? It wants the loving cooperation of the conscious where it's stuck in life.

Let's abbreviate "basic self" as "b/s"

Giving credit where credit is due, the b/s, c/s and h/s abbreviations were invented by Vicki Lacher-Miller, a clairvoyant in the Santa Barbara area, about 1980.

Our c/s is the one trying to do the right thing, at the right time, with the right people, for the right reasons.

The job of the c/s is to make choices and decisions, to learn how to make better decisions; and, ultimately to make healthy decisions for the highest good of all concerned. Your c/s made the decision to pick up this book. The c/s also makes lists including, "Bad people do these kinds of things. . . Good people do these kinds of things . . ."

The c/s has the job of learning cooperation first with the b/s; then later with the high self.

What does the c/s want? Just ask it.

Let's abbreviate "conscious self" as "c/s"

This is the one who knows the plan of your present embodiment, the lessons the soul planned to accomplish and the unresolved issues it planned to address. Your high self is working right now to ascertain the value of this page for you. Its main job, is determining the value of persons, places, resources and experiences for you now.

The high self is more like a bridge than a destination.

The high self will defer to any higher Being who shows up to assist you.

What does the high self want here in 3D? Anything that facilitates personal-spiritual growing, the working out of unresolved disturbances anywhere in the psyche according to what and how much the soul agreed to attempt this embodiment.

Let's abbreviate "high self" as "h/s"

PROOVE to me there is an inner child!

Animals and insects contrasted with humans

Comparing human beings to animals makes the contrast between the three selves much more obvious.

The "higher" capacities humans have over animals can only come from an expanded experience of self. The highest capacity for selfhood animals possess is roughly equivalent to the capacity for selfhood of the human inner child at mental two and younger. With only rare exceptions, animals are stuck at this single selfhood stage, compared to the human conscious self.

The thinking, language and higher emotions, virtually all animals lack, is due to the absence of the two other positions of selfhood possessed by humans. Human experience has at least two additional "dimensions" beyond how animals can experience themselves. These are the conscious and high self "stations" of selfhood.

These additional stations of selfhood in human beings evidence how humankind is not animal, that humans are indeed something more than animals, in terms of selfhood.

Because the single station of selfhood animals possess does not permit objectivity and compare-contrast, in order to make conscious choices, Nature provides animals with hard-wired instincts.

The capacities to compare and to choose supports:

- conscious choice,

- pattern recognition,

- creating of new patterns, and

- permits speech and tool making.

The combination of these, permits rational thinking and feeling; which is in large part, matching thoughts with feelings; and, matching feelings with thoughts.

Our feelings provide us with feedback on our behavior and the behavior of others. From the feedback of our feelings we learn where our behavior; and the behavior of others, is and is not aligned with our needs and values. Animals are not doing this.

Humor, crying with tears, laughing, modesty and

healthy shame, our higher emotions, even the very most evolved domesticated animals have only glimmers of any of these. It's safe to say while animals have feelings, the degree of their feelings and especially higher emotions, pales in comparison to human beings.

Our high self station enables us to have a close, personal connection with our own Divinity, to our own Divine nature. The h/s stands outside of the physical-material world, in a higher frequency than either inner child or conscious self. This is still us, still self; still part of the created psyche, still not soul.

Your soul overshadows and encompasses the three lower selves, hoping to learn something of value each day here on Earth.

The soul is not one of the three selves. It is not bound by conditions the lower three selves are bound by.

The contrast between humans and insects is even more striking than between humans and animals. Insects has the quality of only having a habit body; habits is all they know, all they can do is grow and perform habitual actions and behaviors. The connection we feel with the higher animals, cats, dogs, dolphins, is much less of a distraction when we contrast ourselves with insects: They have a habit body—and not much else. As long as we acknowledge and spend time upgrading our own habit body, we can learn from and retain our brother and sisterhood with the insect kingdom.

Why we need three selves

1. High self

2. Conscious self

3. Basic self (inner child, habit body, immune system)

The whole of Consciousness is too much bandwidth for souls here in 3D–you and I–to grasp and work with effectively. To avoid scaring or embarrassing us, Spirit does us the great favor of narrowing the bandwidth, the scope of Consciousness, we have to engage in and make choices within. The slim section of consciousness where we are asked to make decisions, choices and be responsible to them, is our conscious self awareness.

This limitation of Consciousness down to what the c/s is asked to handle, is exactly analogous to how the visible light range our eyes respond to in "visible light" is a tiny fraction of the entire range of the electromagnetic spectrum.

Our immortal, eternal soul is beingness. Beingness is the ground of our being –er, so to speak. Beingness is our ultimate nature, not imagery, not memory, not knowledge, not passion, not looking handsome or beautiful, not being materially wealthy

Our conscious self in 3D here, is a microcosm in of Spirit "there." Of course, we can still make errors on our income tax. Our conscious self is a limited replica, an artistic representation in miniature, by the Angels, of our soul.

Q: How can I experience soul?

A: Service. Service in hospices around those ready to make their transition back into Spirit is interesting. Listening with all your sensitivities, you are very likely to gain percepts of what leaves when the soul goes. Once it's gone, it's somewhat conspicuous by its absence.

The b/s and c/s as gifts from Spirit to individual souls

Spirit gifts each soul here in 3D with a spiritual being, assigned to arrange things in all the dim regions of consciousness above our middle self. This is called the high self. It only works for the highest good of the individual it is assigned to. It is functionally equivalent to the anthropomorphic concept, Guardian Angel.

Again to support the soul and the limited conscious self, Spirit gifts us with a being, whose job it is to arrange things in the dim regions below the middle self (the sub-and unconscious). This being also works for the highest good of each individual–as best it can given its conditioning. The most neutral name for this second companion is the "basic self" (John-Roger). It goes by many other names, to be listed later.

The best info we have from teachers and students of this is the high self joins a soul around the time the choice is made to re-embody in the physical. The basic self enters shortly after conception to run the metabolism of the fetus and help build the physical body. The soul typically enters on the first breath. The conscious middle self comes into its own only gradually in a series of puberties at the ages of 2-3, 9, 12, 18-21, and 28 (See Habits: Your Habit Body for a full explication of the five puberties).

It is possible to have more than one high self and more than one basic self but this is rare. If you think you have two basic selves, usually something else is going on worth attending to.

The primary value of learning about the 3S is orientation to the nature of your human nature. A map is not the territory; and, the better the map, the easier you can get around.

The three selves as inter-penetrating fields

As we leave behind us the Great Age of the Isolated Intellect, we have some bad habits in our thinking to address. One of them is conceiving of the brain as a set of skills, linked together like tinker toys. Rudolf Steiner pointed out the limitations of this kind of thinking as early as 1890; he called it "part-to-whole thinking."

Part-to-whole is how you build the pyramid at Giza and

assemble cars on an assembly line. But the psyche is NOT composed this way. Linear, bit by bit, synthetic thinking is a poor model of how we think, feel, do and act.

Steiner highlighted whole-to-part thinking as the necessary counterpart, the other half of human thinking processes.

In the 1990s the quantum physics discussion raised again many of the same gaps in Western knowledge the Theosophists and metaphysicians of the 1890s addressed. One of the more fruitful approaches quantum physicists popularized is the idea of inter-penetrating fields.

The clearest clairvoyants say everything in our material world, animate and inanimate, is energy, and radiates energy. The earth is one enormous energy field, a field of fields. The human psyche is a microcosm of this, a configuration of many interacting and inter-penetrating fields. Each individual is a localization (concentration) of energy within larger universal fields.

This is most true of our brains; which like personal computer architecture, functions based on the overlap and convergence of a few thousand smaller programs. In the human being, habits are our operating system. We run and function well only when thousands of habit routines are running. Then we make choices on top of that background and foundation provided by our habit body.

The idea of inter-penetrating fields encompasses both part-to-whole processes and whole-to-part processes and leads us to highlight certain activity:

Metaphor one ~ Swimmer on a summer's day

A swimmer swims in a lake on a pleasant summer's day. She plays, floats on the surface, forms rhythmic strokes, moves around. Above is the Sun, shining warmly down, making all her Earthly pleasures possible. Below, the water buoys her up, holding her up, supp0orting her from below.

The only way she can move forward is to push against the water. It's fun; everyone can do it. She keeps her head above the water, in the sunlight, out of the wet, cool, dim water below. She feels safer, more comfortable, with head above water. She concerns herself with her own actions on the surface--unless a friend pulls her leg and drags her below.

Under water is dim and unfamiliar. Being underwater for short periods is a thrill. She can open her eyes underwater yet visibility is low, dark and hard to see. She can't stay underwater long. She can if she chooses, dive deeper down into the water and swim. If she dives deep enough and stays down long enuf, sometimes fear arises. "Can I survive down here?" In the light, on the surface, it's easier to see and play with other swimmers.

Harder to play with other swimmers underwater.

She knows little about water and less about all that is underwater. That unknowns may exist in the water's depths bothers her occasionally. Mostly she puts such questions out of her mind.

She watches other swimmers in the lake. Some are preoccupied with staying afloat in the water, some with just learning to swim, some preoccupied with swimming technique per se. The Sun warms the water and the swimmer whatever their pursuit.

The swimmer stops and treads water. Gratitude fills her heart to realize the Sun makes all this possible. The Sun warms her, the air and the water. The Sun is not too close, not too bright, which would burn her, nor is it too far, distant and cold. The water too has blessed her. She recalls the miracle of water: two gases that combined are neither so thin as to be vapor nor too mineralized as to be harsh. She holds her hand to her heart and recalls a friend's words, "When you talk gratitude, you are talking with God. She feels protected and enfolded both above and below. Somehow the Universe has loving regard and concern for the welfare of swimmers everywhere. The swimmer is supported both above and below. Everything supports the swimmer in the middle.

Metaphor two ~ A walk in the park

It's a gorgeous blustery March day, minutes after a refreshing watery spring downpour. The park is lush with dancing green foliage. Freshly minted red, yellow and blue flowers turn in the breeze. You notice green reaching up to the sky, Nature yearning for the highest.

The Sun comes out from behind the few remaining clouds, constant and bright. The parkway path is mostly uphill. You don't mind; you like a challenge and know there is nothing on your path you can't handle. Your faithful golden retriever trots beside you obedient and attentive to your every move. No leash is needed. Your dog knows you and ignores all other masters. Your dog loves you and you feel en rapport with it. She sniffs the air sensing everything alive around her. She listens, 360 degrees around her, gathering impressions, as if to say, "What is in play around us today!"

You were smart to bring a warm coat. You thrust your hands into the deep pockets and hug it close. You warm and protect yourself. Your face lifts to the thin gray clouds passing away. The warmth of Father Sun falls on your cheeks. You smile, all is well. Life is good and God is my Partner. You move forward on your path, supported above, below and around by those who love you, known and unknown. The rest of this book on the three selves is no more than commentary on the above.

Metaphor three ~ The three selves

as the three ages of man

The three selves as the three ages of man: young child, adult, experienced grandparent

Hopefully this characterization will assist you to have conversations with your own Three Selves.

Our lower-frequency helper-self, our basic self, our inner child, is analogous to the young child before seven years of age. Waldorf school educators have characterized this developmental stage exceedingly thoroly. For our purposes, the young child makes few distinctions between fairy tales and what adults call "real life." In Fairy Tale Land, the past, present and future are all happening at once with little effective sequencing. The young child converges and identifies with the physical body and the NOW. It is the most attached of the three selves, healthy attachments are supposed to be formed. The young child easily recalls and can give up to Oneness. She does not have responsibility for life-changing decisions.

Our middle self, our waking rational mind--either feeling or thinking-dominant--tries to keep up with what other adults call the "real world;" and of course, this differs somewhat widely depending on local culture. Our conscious self is the most isolated of the three selves so it can focus its efforts on making better choices, what to attach to and what to detach from.

Our high frequency helper-self, our high self, is analogous to an experienced grandmother or grandfather, more wise with age, one foot already reunited with Spirit. Healthy elders understand all three ages, child, adult and other elders. Healthy elders are no longer slaves to the isolation of the mere ego. Our high self is the most detached of our three selves.

The above may cue you to what kind of conversations you are likely to have with each of the Three Selves.

Metaphor four ~

The 3S as computer operating system

If the physical body is the hardware, and

existing psychologies and all therapeutic modalities,

including education,

are the software applications, then

the three selves is our operating system, the "firmware."

The three selves can also be described as a body of habits on all levels, physical, imaginal, emotional, mental, unconscious and soul (PACMES or CIEMUS).

The three selves is the "shell" application within which all sub-programs and choice-making operates. The shell enhances usefulness and connectivity, the ability to get around a large, expanding system. Some readers will recall how Windows began as a "shell" program in exactly this sense.

Without equating human beings too closely with computers, we can take this analogy a teeny step further. Our belief systems, habits and behaviors could then be the "files" produced using this or that set of preferences. The underlying operating system remains neutral to both the preferences it is set for and neutral about the results it is employed to produce.

The above suggests how the three selves could be the first effective "big tent" for 21st century psychology, within which virtually all psychological approaches have common ground and can cross-train usefully.

If any reader can name another psychology with capacity to be the big tent for psychology, I'd sure like to hear about it.

Metaphor five ~ Curious George

The playful young chimpanzee called *Curious George* in the 1941 children's book, Curious George, by H.L. Rey, began a series of books, cartoons and merchandising. Curious George is a healthy representation of the happy basic self. More, the relationship between Curious George and the Man in the Yellow Hat in the first book, depicts the healthy relationship possible between conscious self and inner child.

If you examine a copy of the first book in the series especially, note how the appeal is happiness. The stories are happy, the pictures are happy. Sailors, policemen, everyone--is smiling; the drawing style is simplified, accessible. Yes, most children's books 1940-1975, possess these attributes. Children's books are for the child in all of us.

In the first book George tries to fly like a seagull and falls off an ocean boat and almost drowns. He puts in a false alarm to the fire department. For this he experiences the natural consequence of going to jail. George "steals" a bunch of helium balloons and flies perilously over the city creating a public commotion (and receiving lots of attention). George lands on top of a stop light in a busy intersection and causes a traffic jam, attracting a crescendo of attention. All of these mishaps occur while the Man in the Yellow Hat is out of the picture, all the mishaps occur while George is unmonitored and unsupervised.

The subtext of the first book especially is the healthy, life-affirming relationship between George and the Man. The Man is loving mentor to the curious child-monkey. Despite George's shenanigan's, there no punishment or judgment ever. He does not blame or scold George for his errors. After every mishap, the Man in the Yellow Hat is always happy to have George returned to him.

Nor does the Man blame or scold himself for his lapses in (self) discipline. Without blame either way, the Man turns each problem, each "lemon" into lemonade. This is clearly why George loves the Man. He is fun and uplifting to be with. Curious George is a fable of healthy parenting.

If readers know of a more artistic representation of healthy inner parenting of the basic self by the conscious self, please let me know.

Metaphor six ~ A lit candle

The wax body of a candle represents our somewhat inert physical body well, incorporating the potential for inert matter to become ignited.

The visible candle flame represents our conscious self, the most visible part of the candle, the part that burns brightly, somewhat divorced and apart from the inert physical body but friendly towards it.

The warmest part of a candle flame is not in the visible flame. The warmest part of a flame is invisible and just over the visible flame. This represents the high self very well.

Metaphor seven ~ the 3S as three aspects of music

In *A Wrinkle in Time* the suggestion is made that while

visible things are obvious—invisible things are more real. Music is given as evidence of this. The 3S is another evidence. Music reflects the 3S like this:

dg1

High self	Melody	High frequency
Conscious self	Voice-lyrics	Middle frequency
Basic self	Beat and rhythm	Low frequency

Technically speaking, a successful melody, including many drum lines, is a collaboration between the human and devic/angelic kingdoms.

Esoteric texts specifically ascribe the origins of melody to the angelic realm. This remains the best explanation I've seen for where melody comes from.

Q: HOW does this happen?

A: Spirit is a higher energy potential than 3D. For angels to inspire us with music or other creativity is, for them, like water pouring downhill, from a higher energetic potential to a lower one. It's no effort for them.

The problem is not, "Will we run out of music?" The problem from the angelic point of view is, "Is there anyone down there open to inspiration from above?" If you are open, they can use you.

The 3S as low, middle & high frequency

b/s -- low frequency

c/s -- middle

h/s -- higher frequency

soul -- highest frequency in the individual psyche

In our high frequency self, we are most harmonious and divine. In our low frequency self, we are least harmonious and least divine.

The three selves in popular songs

Many famous pop songs, supposedly expressing sentiments from one lover to another, accidentally or not, express the dynamics between the c/s and b/s.

Billy Joel's classic voice and piano hit song, (Love you) "Just the Way You Are," circa 1986, is written as a young man singing to a young woman. However it also--uniquely--articulates the internal dialog many people have with their own basic self. Here's the one line change to make it a perfect prayer of love and cooperation spoken by conscious to basic self:

I need to know that you will always be

The same old someone that I knew.

What will it take till you I believe in you

The way that you believe in me?

It kills me not to be able to present the full lyrics here. If anyone knows how to work the copyright provisions for song lyrics, I'd love to hear from you. You can access the full lyrics to any song on-line by entering lyrics + (title of song) into Google. Any distribution for pay is prohibited.

So when you view the full lyrics, to get the most out of this song, imagine your c/s in the masculine role and your b/s in the feminine role. If you do, you'll be able to hear this song with new ears.

Approximately 30% of all pop song lyrics played on the radio can be viewed as conversation between conscious and basic self. Country & western songs don't tend to fit this pattern as their lyrics are written too tightly around specific experiences and single "hooks."

Other conscious self to basic self songs -

"Sometimes When We Touch," copyright Dan Hill & Barry Mann.

Conscious self to high self songs

"Here And Now" copyright Luther Vandross

Readers, please DO jot down song lyrics here below, in which you hear inner conversations between the selves here. Then email them in!

What's in your healing toolbox?

The Three Selves is an open source healing project. You are as likely to contribute to it and make it better as I am.

As in any open source code project, there must be tools, the tools must be practical, and people must be able to mix and match tools according to the needs of their own unique personal projects. The same goes for open source healing.

In my own Medical Intuitive practice, I have a large number of "tools." This is not unique to me. Effective counselors, therapists and teachers everywhere have large toolboxes. That's one reason we are effective.

My toolbox will differ from your tool box. Mine is full of techniques, information, protocols, old and new, that lead to solutions, for myself and for the next person who wishes to heal something.

You have to toolbox too. With my hand over my eyes and no peeking, I can tell you some of the tools you have in your box. Like to hear? Some tools in your healing toolbox are:

honesty, courage, love.

Go ahead, check for yourself. Yah, everybody has these tools. I tell you, much of healing is open source. It's not the tools—it's who will use the tools, how much and how often—that counts.

Did you know everybody's courage tool is exactly the same size, shape and weight? You may not be as skilled at using your courage tool as your neighbor is. If you use yours, you will get better with it. You become more skilled at the tools you use most often. That's the nature of all tools.

Some tools are more strategic than others. Attention, intention and choice are the most all-purpose tools in everyone's healing toolbox. "Awareness is healing," as they say.

Some tools everybody has--but they don't know what they are, or how to use them.

Forgiveness is the best example of an under-used tool everyone has. See instructions for how to use forgiveness, not as an affirmation but as a soul action, at HealingCoach.org > Articles > Forgiveness 101 (TM)

Some tools are more complex than courage. These tools require reading, study and training. For instance, Neuro-Linguistic Programming (NLP) and BodyTalk, are both difficult to master from books alone. To add these to a tool box, people take classes.

If you come to a tool in this book you already know how to use, skip that section. If you wish to use that tool more effectively, the three selves can help you orient yourself to understanding that tool and how to use the tool better.

My experience is my understanding of the 3S enhances understanding of any energetic tool I pick up. See if the tool of the 3S works for you too.

.vVv.

3S 100: Why *three* selves???

Q: I'm not broken into three pieces!? Where do you get off saying I am not one self but three?

A: This is the main question. Please also see PROOVE to me there is an inner child (animals vs. humans) above in Summary TWO.

The 3S says, the soul is singular—but the psyche, the personality is manifold, composed of numerous, diverse capacities, each like a facet of one large, coruscating gem.

So just be glad this book is not titled, "Our 3,799 Selves," or "Our 5 Billion and Six Selves."

Consider your PC or Mac. It is not just one program—it's many, working together So are you. We don't prefer to address our parts individually and directly--but we can; technicians do.

Let's look at the presupposition about personality we all grew up with: "I am only one self." Where did we all learn that? Who says an adult is one unified self? It's cultural. It's never questioned. We take "I am one person" as a given.

Who is it who naturally sees adults as monolithic, unified wholes? Small children--and dogs. It's natural for small children to picture adults as majestic, unblemished, monolithic "gods."

From birth to at least age seven, children see adults as "giants;" and, "giants who can do no wrong" (Bradshaw). It's nice to have a child think of you as "able to do no wrong." But you and I as adults know better.

In Western culture, the notion the adult psyche is only and exclusively a singularity of some kind, comes from the 18th and 19th centuries, when the logical sequential mind was just coming onto the stage of Western culture and wasn't feeling secure yet. It helped the logical sequential intellect, in its early decades (1750s), to view adults as one single unified undifferentiated, monolithic personality. This also kept early psychology manageable. Unfortunately this old idea had concrete poured all around it; and, it got locked into our K-12 educational system. The idea that the adult psyche is monolithic is mere cultural fashion--arbitrary.

The question here is, do YOU wish to continue seeing as a child sees? Do you wish to continue viewing yourself and other adults as a child does, if these are indeed the origins of the "only one self" view?

How uniquely we each express, depends on how tolerant you are of inner diversity, to a large degree. Only as children mature, do we learn to tolerate diversity--first inside our self. Around age 9-11 many children try running away from home. I did. Why? For the first time, the child stops seeing adults as monolithic giants. The child sees adults have flaws, see relative truths, sees, "My parents are not perfect." Nine years of age is the classic time, in Waldorf stage-development, when a child breaks thru to a new more complex view of people and relationships: Sometimes the giants are good--sometimes the giant adults are bad. Some giants are good; some giants are bad. The world begins to differentiate.

Then what happens? The child becomes a teenager. Teens easily pick thru--then pick apart, any contradictory qualities adults have and make long lists of adult imperfections. The inner world of the teen becomes a more diverse inner world. If you get a psych degree, you learn how to language this in terms like, "chinks in the armor" or "conflicting sub-personalities."

What happens after high school? If the child is lucky, she grows into committing to committing to Self. She begins a path of personal-spiritual growth. She resonates with teachers who discuss–with integrity-- how the human being is a symphony of many voices, and learns how to conduct and channel her own inner symphony into coherent and purposeful expression.

The human being as made up of many selves has been a cultural undercurrent active "secretly" in personal-spiritual growth circles in the West since Gurdjieff in France, around 1900. The idea of our many selves became increasingly mainstream with:

- Hugh Missildine, M.D.'s *Your Inner Child of the Past* (1963)

- Elizabeth O'Connor's, *Our Many Selves* (1971)

- Fritz Perls' Gestalt dialogs in the middle 1970s,

- Margaret Paul's *Inner Bonding* series,

- Celebration of ethnic diversity in the 1970s and 1980s.

Voice Dialog and Gestalt Therapy both presuppose a fragmented self in need of integrating. This is a fact all conscious selves here in 3D uncover sooner or later at some time on their growth journey. Whether the conscious self takes up the work of Coherence, Integration and Alignment (CIA), is your choice. Most of us need a coach who has gone on ahead of where we are at least somewhat. I'm grateful for my coaches.

Integrating and maturing up are closely related ideas. The young child says, "I am One," and Creation flows out of their oneness. The mature adult says, "I am multitude; this is how Creation flows out of me."

The adult multi-tasks more effectively than the young child. So the snake bites his tail: At some point the multitude of inner parts, inner selves must be presided over and given direction by a single voice, and choose one allegiance and not another, ride one horse at a time, not two, etc.

The conscious self is indeed the captain of its own "ship" of the three selves, each c/s ultimately responsible for the ship's direction and all choices made on board. This reflects the singularity of the soul.

Making distinctions is part and parcel of growing

Making distinctions is part and parcel of personal-spiritual growth. You have to make new distinctions in your own psyche as you grow, or you become stuck

The human being is NOT a unified field. 19th

philosophy and 20th century consumerism persuaded us we are each an isolated island, a unified field. The 3S shows this is *not* so; we are only an "island" in the most limited physical-material sense.

Our lone, single, unitary, island self, is our conscious self; it mirrors our identity as a soul.

Our basic self, also called, the habit body, immune systems and so on, is our ally *below* the conscious self. Our high self is our ally *above* the rational mind.

The conscious self, reflecting the soul, is the chooser and the decider. Soul is choice. Every team needs a captain to focus decision-making.

Whether we are cerebral dominant or gut brain dominant, the dilemma is the same. Trying to live our life from the goal of avoiding pain is not a path to freedom. The pained part will only ever have a partial picture of the highest good. Partnership with the b/s, c/s and the Light is the way to go.

v\V/v

Chapter 3S 101:

The whole human psyche

A clarifying term for all 21st century psychology:
healthy

If we drop the obsession with physical and psychological
pathology, the obsession of the 18th thru 20th
centuries--what will we talk about in health care? What
do you talk about if sickness and illness are no longer
your focus?

Health, optimal wellness, and becoming fully human.
When the 3S are aligned, all looking the same direction,
all seeing and moving towards the same goal, there is
inner harmony, Coherence, Integration, Alignment, even
a feeling of spiritual marriage, all the parts become one.
That's inner health.

dg2

What is 'One Whole' in psychology?

What is 100% of psychology? What is the sum of all
human potential, all human potentials possible, from in-
utero to final breath, of anyone who has ever lived?
What does it means to be fully human here in 3D here
and now?

18th and 19th century psychology are great examples

of how far you can go into a rut if you fail to find a good starting point, if you fail to compose clear questions to investigate the unknown. All fruitful explorations into unknowns formulate good questions at the beginning. This often takes time and effort. Worth it.

If psychology had stuck with the larger questions of human existence as their starting point, boy would things be different today.

We're not looking for any answers yet. We're still working on clarifying our starting place. The following diagrams

suggest WHY we have three selves. There is so much going on, one awareness on one level is not enuf to handle it all.

Let one circle represent ALL of what it means to be fully human

dg3

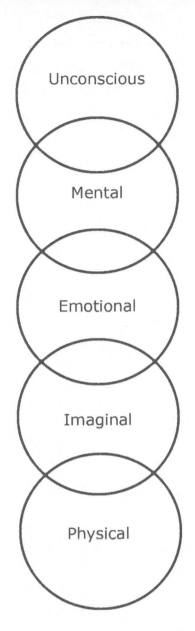

If it is something a human being ever has done or can do now, it's in this circle.

Notice our circle is dashed, broken, permeable. The human psyche is semi-permeable. Humanity is evolving and growing. Humanity is changing over time.

HealingToolbox.org

Five vehicles or bodies to get around in 3D

To navigate around in physical-material worlds, the soul--not pictured above--requires a vehicle or body on each level to be awake on that level. No body on a level equals no awareness on that level. If you prefer to think about these as five distinct octaves, fine. It can also be a rainbow where the colors are distinct AND they all join hands.

You can demonstrate the reality of the five vehicles you are using here now in 3D quite easily. A famous exercise from the early 1970s says

Close your eyes. Quiet your physical body...

Quiet your imagination...

Quiet your emotions...

Quiet your mind...

Quiet your memories and habits...

Now who's doing all that? Who's doing the quieting?

You, the eternal, immortal part of you, the soul.

In our diagrams, this divine active aspect of you is not shown. Think of your divine creative part as permeating all your levels.

Picturing personal-spiritual growth

Each of us has an inner experience of "me." This is our little zone of comfort. That's the little inner circle below, where we are awake in our little comfort zone.

dg4

The larger circle around the smaller here represents the sense we always have "room to grow." There is always more potential we could grow into we haven't done yet.

"Me" and "psyche" are synonymns here. The small circle is our comfort zone within the full expanse of our psyche.

Below the little circle of "me" is shown distributed over the PACME levels of human potential. Note the ample room to grow on each level. Each semicircle shows the partial awareness the little circle "me" has on each level. Put the semicircles back together and you have the drawing above again.

The larger circle is everything human the individual could be, if he or she expanded optimally in all directions.

(4) This next diagram is the same information as diagram 3. The large circle is "everything potential in an individual psyche." Now the larger circle is also divided into PACME. The little circle of "me, what I manifest" is now "spread out" over the bigger one, suggesting how much potential it has manifested on each level PACME.

dg5

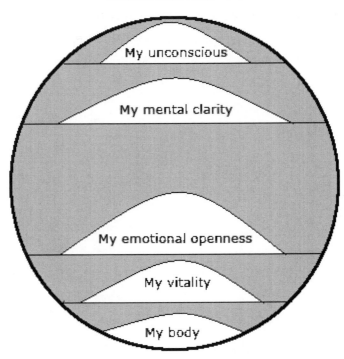

If you put the semicircles back together, you'll have the little me circle in Diagram 3 again.

Any individual we diagram in this way will have their own unique "distribution" of manifested potential. No matter who they are, they will still be ample room to grow.

As you increase your energetic strength, your aura gets brighter—and in the diagram, the circle of your psyche increases its diameter.

The above diagrams suggest what's going on in just one human psyche. Given this complexity, can you imagine the sense it makes, why the soul might have use for three beings to assist it in managing all this activity?

Without adequate and sufficient spiritual assistance, from both below and above, the soul would be perpetually bogged down simply stabilizing and maintaining its bodies PACME. It would have little time for anything else!

u/U\u

3S 102: Into the etheric

The problem ain't with what people know. The problem is with what people know *that tain't so*; that's the problem -~Josh Billings, circa 1930s

-=+=-=+=--=+=- -=+=- -=+=--=+=- -=+=- -=+=-

Being a scientist is simply being careful not to fool yourself -- John Carlson, amateur rocket scientist

-=+=--=+=- -=+=- -=+=--=+=- -=+=- -=+=-

What would happen if we took Ernest Holmes, founder of Religious Science, at his word: The thing we are searching for is the thing we are searching with. Holmes would have our inner experience not only be the object of discovery; it must be the tool of discovery as well. -- Unknown

-=+=-=+=--=+=- -=+=- -=+=--=+=- -=+=- -=+=-

Psychology means "soul knowledge." It means the study of the spirit, but it has never been that. Psychology [instead became] the study of cognitions, perceptions and [emotional] affects. It [became] the study of the personality -- Gary Zukav, *The Seat of the Soul*, Ch. 13 p 193-4

-=+=-=+=--=+=- -=+=- -=+=--=+=- -=+=- -=+=-

Right here we have to face right up front the difficulty of our topic. The three selves is real--but it is so simple, it cannot be grasped with sequential logic.

Don't define – characterize"

In a lop-sided culture based on only the logical sequential intellect, etheric phenomena remains a cultural blind spot. The etheric is above the mind in frequency, more subtle yet. Only fragments of what happens in the etheric has an analogue in the mind. The mind gets confused trying to understand the etheric on mental terms alone.

The analogous, more familiar problem, is trying to compose a clear mental picture of feelings. This exposes the partialness with which thoughts can be used to explain feelings.

In the mind, everything is laid out in discrete, separate pieces. Butterflies pinned and displayed on a board inside a glass case.

Above the mind, things run together, moosh together. We are on our way back to Oneness, where everything is mooshed together.

The problem is the etheric is too alive, too organic, dynamic, continually weaving and mixing, where every "object," upon closer inspection, is a crossroads, a confluence and convergence of many streams of creation. This overwhelms the merely mental in us.

Rudolf Steiner's advice works best, forget about naming, labeling and categorizing live phenomena, prefer always to characterize living things.

The etheric is connectivity itself

The 3S is simpler than sequential logic, prior to sequential thinking. Sequential logic connects thing to thing to thing, one by one, in a linear sequence. Connectivity is everything at once, or virtually so.

Recently I realized before there was right and wrong, there was only loving. This is why lovemaking with a cherished partner is so much fun; neither party can do anything "wrong."

There are three selves but they are not in a linear

sequence; they are more of a whole, more of a system. This is how the human psyche can be of one whole, thru connectivity. This is how our brain can be of one whole, thru connectivity.

All brains function thru connectivity

If our brain did not function primarily thru connectivity; then, the human brain would function with less intelligence than a modern desktop computer. Increased connectivity is precisely what separates stiff, 1950s era robotic computers from Windows XP and beyond. Microsoft probably calls this inter-connectivity or multi-media, but you get the idea: connectivity. Just like in the living human brain.

If you try to grasp the three selves solely with your linear, sequencing intellectual mind, you can give up now and save yourself a lot of frustration.

The word "ether" comes from the Greek, meaning to light up or kindle. When seen by clairvoyants it's seen as luminous substance. Like the basic self, etheric energy has many names:

- The Chinese call it li, the unifying principle

- Chi then is the energy flowing in the li.

- Prana is another word for chi.

- Life-force, Bio-energy,

- bioplasma, a usefully descriptive Soviet word.

As this etheric substrate permeates all 3D substance, it is in a good position to coordinate life functions, enabling individuals to function as coordinated units, which it does. The etheric body is in a good position to enable every part to interact and communicate with every other part, and so it does: "The Web that Has No Weaver."

This invisible etheric counterpart of each and every living cell and keeps it alive. When the etheric body withdraws from the physical, death occurs, for the cells no longer receive the necessary cosmic vitality thru the etheric web of life, the web permeating the whole of creation.

The distribution of vital force to the physical cell appears to go thru the mitochondria, the cell's power house. If so this suggests the mitochondria perform the analogous function in cells to the spleen chakra in the whole human being (this paragraph revised and paraphrased from an unknown web discussion of the four ethers, excerpted July 2002).

Owen Waters at InfiniteBeing.com uses the term "pre-physical body." This is another term for the etheric body, especially appropriate for the four lower sub-ethers of warmth, reactivity, light and crystallization. For more on this, see "Girls jump UP; Boys jump DOWN" in the Appendices of Volume Two.

Your mind cannot grasp ONE

Because the three selves behave primarily as a unit, trying to touch and hold them altogether is like trying to touch and hold the number ONE. You can do many things with the mind; and, you can write "1;" but, the only way to experience ONE is thru intuition and that's above the mind.

You understand ONE with the part of you that is ONE. That part is above the mind. So understanding the three selves requires using a part of you big enuf to encompass all three selves. The mind tries but the soul does. To understand ONE with the mind, you come back to the subject over and over, learning more and more aspects of it. This over and over gesture is sometimes called recursiveness.

John-Roger's contribution to the 3S

A continuing source of interest in the three selves is John-Roger, an educator and speaker, founder of an ecumenical church, the Movement of Spiritual Inner Awareness. See msia.org, forgive.org, or LovingEachDay.org for more. His presentation of the three selves in the 1970s and 1980s was a major event in the field of psychology, in my opinion, beginning the process of redeeming psychology from its *X-Files* cum

LOST state and false starts in the 18th thru 20th centuries.

J-R extended understanding of the 3S far beyond the research of Max Freedom Long. Evidence strongly suggests J-R can both b/ss and h/ss directly so this is quality information. A classic recording of his seminal San Francisco 3S seminar is available at msia.org. The number of doors J-R opened in this field are so numerous, we make no attempt to explore all of them in even both volumes of the present work.

Intellect vs. Intelligence

Since the Quantum discussion of the 1990s, all our most forward thinkers and researchers are pretty sure the mind is *not the top* of the human psyche. Unless they know about etheric formative forces and how the etheric has both lower frequency phenomena (vitality, acupuncture meridans, etc) and higher frequency phenomena (the mythological level of Divine Feminine, Divine masculine, the Horn of Plenty, The Void, etc). They are not too sure exatly *what* is above the mind, the intellect, but they know *something* is present and active.

One thing above the logical-sequential mind, the mere intellect, is intelligence.

Joseph Chilton-Pearce, in a cassette tape on his magical Child topic, points out a cultural confusion. We equate the logical-sequential mind—intellect—with intelligence. He says it's quite easy to make a useful distinction between the two.

The intellect works in logical sequential ordering. It prefers consistent logic, no matter where it leads.

Intelligence is holistic, is not linear, expects things to be holograms, every part affecting all other parts.

Making connections to consequences beyond only scientists, is intelligence at work. Seeing patterns that affect beyond only scientists, is intelligence at work. Making choices aligned with the greatest good for the greatest number, is intelligence at work, working for The Whole.

Intellect stops with the mind. Intelligence is a soul capacity. The soul is intelligent, not intellectual.

If you're thinking Big Oil and GMO patenting tend to be intellect and ecology, environmentalism and sustainability tend to be intelliegence; then, you re on to something.

Pearce says in his lectures that an intellect can design an atomic bomb but only intelligence can come to the conclusion the use of any bomb is not aligned with human values. Indeed it is only intelligence that realizes the whole endeavor of bomb making is against human values; that, responding to aggression with more aggression has a very poor track record. This exercise of intelligence is soul in action.

The ego using the intellect tends to despise the etheric. The mind knows, "This is where I meet my Waterloo." Shifting, weaving, converging and diverging currents in the etheric defeat sequential logic. That's why so many definitions of the unconscious have been formulated-- and so few agree. Only those definitions that try to characterize the etheric are likely to agree. The metaphor "womb of creation" points to the dynamic quality of the etheric. "Womb of creation," doesn't that sound like more than mere mind can accomplish? One of the first things infants do is begin making connections in their brains, associate things and percepts.

More common than patterns in the etheric are rhythms, hence music is of the etheric.

Experience unknown energies right now!

Heck, you can prove the existence of energies unknown to material science right now: stand sideways to a sturdy wall with one arm and shoulder against the wall. Try as hard as you can to lift your arm against the wall for a count of 50. Stand away from the wall, relaxing your arm. What happens?

This interesting phenomena is not directly related to

etheric forces. It falls in the discussion of levity and gravity, a Rudolf Steiner topic, beyond our scope here.

So if you feel like you are losing your mind, you are getting what we are saying.

The objective of etheric energies is to vitalize, energize and coordinate all levels conditioned existence.

Experience your etheric body right now

Want to experience your etheric body right now? Easy. Just stand up and spin in place ten times. Now stop. The woozy effect is your etheric body being slightly out of alignment with your physical body. The changing wooziness is your e-body righting itself back into optimal relationship with your physical body again.

Want to experience the quality of the etheric right now? Think of any two rhyming words you like or poetry with rhymes you like. Rhymes achieve their interest and energy from the etheric. The etheric is the realm of repeating and repeating and repeating with slight changes and transformations. We have a word for slight changes and transformations. That word is evolution. The etheric expresses as evolution in the rhythm of change at different levels.

The amoeba-like behavior of our etheric body

An easy way to recognize the activity of the etheric body is to walk down the street and watch someone attractive of the opposite sex. If you are relaxed, you will naturally find a part of you goes out to them. That's the etheric body going out there. Remind yourself that it's unethical to undress someone mentally and bring all of yourself back to your self. What is coming back to you? That's your etheric body coming back home.

The human etheric body (David Tansley)

The etheric body has three basic functions, all closely interrelated. It acts as a receiver of energies, an assimilator of energies and as a transmitter of energies [on all conditioned levels]. If each of these functions is maintained in a state of balance, then the physical body reflects the interchange of energies as a state of good health. ...the etheric body is the instrument of life which produces and sustains the physical form. It is the true intermediary and unseen link between the physical world and the subjective realms of the astral [and above]. Upon its correct reception and distribution of energies, depends the health of the physical body (*Radionics and the Subtle Anatomy of Man* (1972) p. 18-22. Not recommended reading)

The above is how the Theosophical-metaphysical generations talked about the inner child before John Bradshaw's presentation in the 1980s.

Find the etheric in chemistry between lovers

In the dating scene, participants often say, "There has to be chemistry between us." Is "chemistry" real or only another romantic illusion? Chemistry is indeed real, as anyone who has felt it can tell you. But what is it? Astrology clarifies "chemistry" as magnetic potentials, cross-referenced with the different categories of etheric substance. Astrology for people can also be called the study of magnetic potentials in the basic self.

Find the etheric in Zen

The etheric realm will be familiar to many readers as the realm of the Zen koan, the realm of "neither this nor that." That's why the yin-yang symbol has a little spot of white in the black tadpole and a little spot of black in the white tadpole. It's a flowing, weaving realm wherein lies the "womb of creation." Consequently, the inner child, cannot be grasped altogether with the conscious mind. The mind can only grasp glimpses–just like all of Zen Buddhism says.

"We are all living in an energy field that unites the seen and unseen universe" (David Hawkins). If this were NOT so, then there would already be many comprehensive textbooks on the inner child.

Thru reading and study, you do catch glimpses. One facet show itself, you keep looking into different facets; eventually, the inner child shows up in your own personal experience. Once you recognize your own inner child, book learning becomes secondary. You have had an EXPERIENCE of the inner child and know where to go to get another experience with him or her or it. Always go for the experience!

vVv

Chapter 3S 103: Frequently Asked Questions

Q: What does the conscious self want?

A: Without wisdom, the c/s wants only what the small "s" self, the ego, wants. With more wisdom, the c/s wants to make good choices, healthy choices, the right thing to do, with the right people, at the right time, for the right reasons, to paraphrase Aristotle; hence, "What is for the highest good here?"

Q: What does the basic self want?

A: Unless the conscious self gets involved, the b/s wants to preserve its comfort zones and make them bigger.

From the angle of personal-spiritual growth, the b/s wants better cooperation with the c/s towards mutual goals. Happiness is the accumulation, the sum, of many individual healthy choices. The basic self knows this, understands very well how lousy choices make its comfort zone smaller—but it is not in charge, in the healthy person.

The "enlightened" basic self wants the c/s to get busy, take responsibility for making 3D life better and more comfortable, to pay attention to dysfunctional habits no longer working and redirect them. The b/s wants the c/s to be a wise, nurturing parent who will address, redeem and upgrade things that aren't working too well into habits, behaviors and routines that work better for all three selves.

Courage comes into play here because for the c/s to change direction on a longstanding habit many times means it has to put up with whining and complaining of the b/s as lets go of old habit patterns and adjusts to new routines, the "teach an old dog new tricks" syndrome.

Q: What does the high self want?

A: The high self doesn't want anything for itself that I have ever seen; it wants to be of service to the two lower frequency selves. It has a definite preference for the c/s to spend perhaps 15 minutes or more a day "looking upward" towards spirit in any ritual-form-method the c/s prefers. The high self wishes the c/s would upgrade its decision-making ability so it makes healthy choices more often. If you have the luxury of time, asking for second opinions often leads to better decisions—as long as we are entering into "paralysis by analysis." When the c/s slows down and invites the h/s to contribute a second opinion on a specific question, the more the h/s feels included and acknowledged.

\v\V/v/

Chapter 3S 104:

A brief history of playfulness

Growing up is the hardest job anybody ever has to do
~ John Bradshaw

It takes courage to grow up and turn out to be who you really are ~ e.e. cummings

This chapter aims to establish the mood of playfulness the three selves operates in; and, remind readers, who did not live thru it, about the significant history of playfulness, the era roughly 1965-1975.

The 3S works best in the mood of playfulness. Heck, all learning works best in the mood of relaxation (John Morton). Surprisingly little psychological literature and activity addresses this. The exceptions, Carl Rogers, Eric Berne, Virginia Satir, Bandler & Grinder, John Thie, created about the only modalities still vibrantly alive today. The 3S that comes out of the fun and joy of personal-spiritual growth, started as an outsider too. If you want to learn what the mood of the later 1960s and early-mid 1970s was all about, read on!

Polarity: Seriousness and Playfulness

Seriousness and self-discipline are essential at many points in growth. All major 20th century psychologies suggest this. However, play is also crucial. In the therapy innovations of the 1970s, the pendulum of Western culture moved towards playfulness, correcting the excess Seriousness of the 1900s-1960s, in the study of the psyche.

Find an artistic image of this cultural transformation in the Tom Hanks, Robert Zemekis movie Forest Gump. Young Forest, mentally slow, believes himself to be a cripple. He wears heavy metal leg braces, has worn them since he was a child. In 1958, for the first time, he hears Elvis Presley play his guitar and sing an upbeat song. His joy liberates him to run! He runs so far and so fast, he literally runs his braces off his legs. This suggests the magnitude of joy and change in the national character in the U.S. in the 1960s and 1970s. I call this the great leap forward. When the cultural pendulum got unstuck from the 1950s and 1960s, it came unstuck with a bang!

The two sides of an old quarter, 25 cents

To switch metaphors, Seriousness and Playfulness are two sides of the coin of freedom. Until recently, George

Washington on one side of the quarter, an eagle in flight on the other. You can only have as much fun and freedom as you have of honesty and self-discipline. The two grow together in healthy people. These are the two sides of the coin of the number five in numerology.

The Playfulness - Seriousness polarity is also articulated in Meyers-Briggs Type Indicator (MBTI) as the P-J split:

P = sPontaneity, expansion, laughter, frivolity, and imProvization, "Aloha," as subjectively determined.

J = closure, resolution, accountability, integration, groundedness, pre-planning, structure, form, rehearsal, orderly growth, "Goodbye," as subjectively determined (old: Judging).

We need both. Fun (P) is more likely if we make and work towards goals (J); without bouts of free play (P), how would any of us relax from the most serious work of all, growing up, maturing ourselves (J)? A spirit of play makes work worthwhile.

Perhaps some day a book will be written called The Playful and the Promethean, a longer history of playfulness. It might start like this:

Playfulness prior to the 1960s

Prior to the late 1960s, the mood of Seriousness prevailed, fostered by IQ tests, two world wars, unnecessary use of nuclear power and the dark and unhappy ruminations and analysis of conventional Freudian psychotherapy, born in the 1890s.

The first wave of healthy playfulness in the 20th century was probably Surrealism, in the 1920s. The next wave was probably the social awakening of the 1960s culminating in the tidal wave of hippie, flower child, cultural alternatives flowering between 1965 and 1975.

It's instructive to list the other minor waves of healthy playfulness:

- Stand up comedy and improv schools, begun in the 1970s

- Psychodrama (born in the 1920s, caught on in the 1970s)

- Gestalt Therapy, often coupled with Transactional Analysis in the 1970s

- Whole Earth Catalog crew (1970s)

- "New Games" and PlayFair, 1970s and 1980s

- Play therapy and art therapy, mostly for very young and severely traumatized kids (early 1970s)

- Orff-Schulwerk, music, drama and dance improvisation for all ages (developed in Europe in the 1950s, caught on in the US in the 1970s)

- "Free schools," even some kid-run schools in the 1960s, 1970s and late 1990s (not a recommended school model but significant here),

Contact Improvisation and avant garde dance (exploded in the 1970s).

Storytelling (last seen in the 1930s, revived 1970s)

Traditional crafts, traditional dances (contra, English etc), and Renaissance Fairs.

All of these encourage, even require relaxed fun and experimentation.

Fads are how Spirit renews itself in the 3D world

To understand Surrealism, TA and some of the other activity mentioned above, it will help to digress to a short consideration of fads. This will also help you if you wish to start a fad. You can start a fad in a single school if you have heart and tune in to what the unconscious needs are.

A healthy fad is good. Most healing modalities travel thru our culture in fad-like manner, like a wave, borne forward by the enthusiasm of individuals like you. Fads is a prime way Spirit renews itself here on Earth. How else could Spirit brings new impulses to enliven this level, where comfort, security, sameness and inertia rule. Virtually all new healthy impulses become known initially thru fads.

Unhealthy fads exist also: smoking cigarettes for one. "Fashion" exists and can also be healthy or unhealthy.

Transactional Analysis (TA) was a textbook example of a healthy fad. TA was the first coupling of personal growth with play and healthy activity. Prior to TA, in the mainstream, all psychotherapy was in the mood of pathology, death and disease. Carl Rogers and a group therapy entered the mainstream primarily after TA broke the ice.

Berne's framing of serious personal dilemmas as non-threatening games, brought these behaviors out of the closet for open discussion. Indeed, TA was the beginning of bringing serious personal issues" out of the closet" into social conversation.

In TA, it's OK, par for the course, and very ordinary, to be involved in dysfunctional games with other people. We all do it! Berne had fun teaching people how to have fun becoming aware of these unhealthy games and undoing the Games People Play.

To understand how TA became a fad sweeping up the media, many individuals and pockets of people across the U.S., we have to understand how the wave formed.

Many readers will know lay-person psychology revolution has its roots with Carl Rogers in the 1940s, T-groups (therapy groups) at Harvard in the late 1940s, and early group therapy, in the immediate WW II postwar period. Mainstream culture turned a blind eye also to much creative activity occurring in Waldorf schools in the 1950s and to "experimental schools" in the 1960s.

A large fraction of the public was ready for TA's message of play, bringing it back as a valued part of the psyche. Play was *proven* useful; the experts said so!

TA was the beginning of the coaching phenomenon we know today: no one is "broken;" there is only self-improvement from wherever you are today.

Before TA was on TV and magazine covers, TA and group therapy had been spreading rapidly underground among professional psychiatrists, despite lack of mainstream recognition, absence of literature and no best sellers.

Then Berne's books hit the stores. A series of best selling books brought this new psychological wealth and know-how out in the open to laypersons. Breakout bestsellers by other authors brought wide attention to Berne's developments,

I'm OK-You're OK by Thomas Harris M.D. in 1968, *Why Am I Afraid To Tell You Who I Am?* by John Joseph

Powell, 1969, and a handful of others. *Born to Win: Transactional Analysis with Gestalt Experiments by* James & Jongeward was another highlight and a very impressive publishing phenomena.

Another reflection of the time, *The Inner Game of Tennis* (first ed 1970s) made growth a game, upgrading your game, being more on top of your game. Contrast this with Depth Psychology (Freud, Adler, Jung) which dominated psychotherapeutic thinking 1890-1960 with deep intellectual analysis. Depth psychology was expert-driven.

TA broke down the walls academia and professional societies had built up between experts and the public. TA was close up, hands-on, the beginning of the end for passive analysis on a couch. Experts were de-emphasized. With TA you could now work on yourself directly and uniquely. For the first time, "do your own thing" (for good or ill) was encouraged. TA gave lay persons, with no formal training, pictures and diagrams of interactions for people to understand their own everyday interactions.

TA spread thru counselors sharing TA ideas with clients and groups, who then began to solve some of their own problems. The idea began to catch on. For a significant fraction of the population, direct personal experience and thinking for your self became the standard, not imitating the past, not the authoritative voice of experts.

Eric Berne was a classically trained Freudian psychiatrist. He claims not to have heard of Long's work on Huna when he published his first TA book in 1961. Even if the two are technically unrelated, TA parallels the spirit of playfulness and freedom his contemporary Long experimented in. TA enthuses with good cheer about exploring the diverging voices inside us. Both Long and Berne encourage readers to view personal growth as an adventure. The idea that you could read a book and begin a personal adventure, a journey of growth, was a big part of Max Freedom Long's 23 volumes on Huna. But in the mainstream culture of 1968, this was brand new. Until then all psychology was the exclusive province of white-coated experts. People were ready for a change.

TA's message was a revolution in the field, covered extensively on radio, television, books and magazines. TA books were bestsellers. A large demographic of people willing to grow was identified and brought to light, people willing to reach beyond the comfortable but limiting campfires of the 1950s, willing to explore the dim areas below conscious awareness. Lay people began to network, using grassroots strategies spread widely in the civil rights era. Grassroots involvement continued in the 12-step program boom of the 1980s and in energetic healing and Nonviolent Communication today.

In the early 1970s, led by democratic-minded psychology professionals, brigades of lay persons were trained to take hold of new psychological tools for growth. Local people moved these tools out into their local communities.

The best example known to me is the Southern California Counseling Center, in the Fairfax district of L.A. (on Pico just east of Fairfax), where many therapists still train in 1:1 and group therapy. Two psychiatry professionals began training 50 housewives. They trained each other in how to grow with the tools of TA offered coupled with anything else that worked in the humanistic vein. SCCC remains a thriving community today.

From a 3S point of view, many conscious selves were now strong enough in thinking independently to go beyond "taking on authority" and begin to explore the further inner reaches of their own psyches. People began to talk about moving from "external locus of control" to "internal locus of control." In a real sense this was a maturing up and expansion of the collective inner self. It's the helpless and inadequate, who crave authority, experts and gurus.

With more personal confidence, we do for ourselves more, we want to do for ourselves more. Hence the famous TV commercial of the 1970s, "Mother please! I'd rather do it myself!" which became a catch phrase for the next decade. This maturation was securely in place by 1985 permitting large numbers of psychiatry clients to step out of a medical pathology paradigm taking precedence over experts, rules and dogma. This sea change broke into the cultural mainstream in the late 1960s and defines much of the significance of the famous '60s counter-culture that swept thru creating a loose demographic of "cultural creatives."

This no-fault, try-it-and-see-what-happens approach is crucial to keeping the fun in personal growth. Advancements in growth soon make their way into the wider culture. The phrases "hands-on," self-help," and "user-friendly" are slang first used in 1970s psychology.

"Hands-on," "self help" and "do it yourself" unfolded in the 1970s in the most sensory and materialistic field imaginable: home improvement. Mr. do-it-yourself, J. Baldwin from Whole Earth Review, and Whole Earth Catalog, made the cover of TIME magazine in 1974. The article covers the do-it-yourself revolution with pictures of Sears and Roebucks, where tools and building materials were being advertised and sold directly to home owners, in the way we know it today, for the first time. This was new. Prior to 1970s Sears, to get work done on your home, you had to hire a contractor, hire an expert, or be an expert, to get work done. There were virtually no do-it-yourself. Sears in the 1970s was the ancestor of Home Depot and other home do-it-yourself stores. Slogans like, "You can do it. We can help" the 2003 advertising motto of Home Depot, were unheard of prior to 1970.

The TIME magazine article points out the do-it-yourself,

hands-on, user-friendly hardware revolution, was preceded by similar advances in psychology and psychiatry. First an innovation in human growth--then it devolves to Sears. That's progress. We now take the wide availability of modern self-help books completely for granted.

The surge of popular interest in psychology created by TA, directly spawned the magazine Popular Psychology, a late-comer to the field, around 1974. The same time period spawned East-West Journal the parent of New Age Journal. This activity expanded and became self-help shelves in bookstores in the 1970s. In 2003 the self-help shelf has grown in most stores to two aisles.

I'm no TA expert but I think it's fair to say self-help entered psychology thru TA. The contributions of Gestalt, Esalen and psychodrama while still significant, are more difficult to assess and discuss. The best-sellers, Games People Play (Berne, 1964) and I'm OK, You're OK (Harris, 1968) were the first time psychology made practical sense to a national audience, became meaningful for non-experts.

TA's three semi-independent states of awareness

Berne's three states improved on the abstract urgings delineated by Freud's model of id, ego, super-ego. Freud's "complexes" and "compulsions" clearly had validity but led students away from practical solutions and back into philosophy.

TA modeled behavior as three interacting living beings-- Child, Parent, Adult. TA did little to develop these, focusing on their main use, uncovering and exposing dysfunctional games and habits. Berne was practical: Which self was doing what with which other self, why, and was it healthy or not?

Something else TA got right was using simplified, user-friendly concepts and diagrams. It employed clear and simple diagrams to chart personal interactions, an early graphical user interface (GUI) for psychology. The circles of PAC, and the happy face that evolved from them (in San Francisco in the early 1970s) were a joyful release from the abstract, complex, laborious, intellectually muscle bound theories of Depth Psychology (Freud, Adler, Jung pre-1975). TA replaced pathology terms--with games. Gestalt and psychodrama replaced diagnosing pathology with direct experience and awareness now. TA made psychology fun. Everyone could take part. Learning and doing were together again in psychology (the school system was never able to follow here, another story).

What do You Say after You Say Hello? TA's next bestseller, came out in June 1972. It had five hardback printings and 12 paperback printings by 1973. Hello starts with the most accessible of topics, "How do we say "Hello?" Different kinds of 'hellos' are described. Then the different forms of handshakes are discussed. Psychiatry was brought to Earth--emphatically. Berne explains family of origin dynamics in a simple expository manner. Where Virginia Satir had explained family dynamics usefully for therapists, Berne was able to take this wisdom, couch it in pictures, and talk about dysfunctional behavior as "games." Even street people could get this, and they did.

To paraphrase Henry Ford, TA said whether you think growth is Serious or Playful—you're right!

TA said the lab is life. "Berne's interest was in curing people rather than 'making progress.' He talked about pausing before entering a group, to ask himself the question, 'How can I cure everyone in this room today?'" (Goulding & Goulding 1979 p 4). TA gave hope to the hundreds of thousands of people who had endured dysfunctional relationships in the 1950s and 1960s. TA offered ordinary people simple understandings and tools to undo the damage of their dysfunctional relationship games. TA's advice was hopeful, "Forget about your past. Here's how you change" (from Paul DeSena in conversation). All of this was new at the time.

In the 1980s, when John Bradshaw, NLP and Tony Robbins demonstrated how people could facilitate their own growth, pathology-oriented medical-style psychiatrists began to be replaced with coaches, professionals who try to stay eye-to-eye with clients.

"Death" of TA

Note how Berne's three ego states do not coincide well with basic self, conscious self and high self. However, the two sets of terms are related:

dg6

TA states compared to 3S states in TA

Adult:	Neutral, objective Rational self	High self:	Our psyche above the rational mind, Intuition.
Parent	Parenting habits From early caregiversHabits	C/s:	The choice-making self.
Child	Reactive, Emotional self, Game-player	Basic self:	Reactivity, receptivity, metabolic Functions, Habit body PACME

After Berne, in the 1980s the cultural pendulum swung back towards seriosity. The shortcomings of TA had become apparent. Like all the rest of conventional 20th psych and psychotherapy, it was inherently superficial: wedded to an implicit atheism, "there is no God."

In the 1980s "grounding" became meaningful to reduce excesses of "do your own thing." Spiritual growth could no longer be pursued without being grounded. Once grounded, the "spiritual revolution" took up where the "psychotherapeutic revolution" left off in the 1970s.

The swing back to Seriousness in the 1980s was healthy in many ways too. The youthful "rediscovery of the self" in the 1970s gave way to more mature approaches of the 1980s. Bradshaw was much more serious than TA. In psychology, Cognitive psychology and later, healthy permutations of behavioral psychology added needed rigor and precision to 1:1 and group therapy. "Homework" for clients to complete on their own became popular, perhaps most notably in Brief Therapy.

Improvization is the highest human creativity

Around 2000, the first noises were heard again in psychology that maybe the pendulum had swung too far back to Seriosity. Perhaps the spirit of healthy social play is alive in too few places. Personal and spiritual growth can--and maybe should again--resemble comedy improv.

Correcting and expanding Bloom's taxonomy

Given what we learned in the 1970s, Bloom's Taxonomy can now be improved upon.
Highest order thinking competencies
[Improvization]
Evaluation
Synthesis
Analysis
Application

Comprehension

Knowledge

Lowest order thinking competencies

From Benjamin S. Bloom, *Taxonomy of Educational Objectives*, Allyn and Bacon, Boston, MA. 1984 Pearson Education.

If Improvization is added either above Synthesis or above Evaluation (the process of Evaluation and Improvization is recursive) in his model, then we have something more human. Improvization is a higher order human capacity than Synthesis, which is always imitative to some degree.

The primary modern speakers for the three selves, Max Freedom Long, John-Roger, and Margaret Paul, all approach the topic improvizationaly in large part. Working on yourself or on clients is always partly improvizational.

Bloom's Taxonomy can be further improved by realizing the psyche is not a linear system; it's a matrix of connections, like in our brain.

Danger of moral relativism

Freedom is indeed a two-edged sword and can be abused. Too much hurts as badly as too little. Many of us had friends with lives ruined due to drugs and/or irresponsibility. "Do your own thing" is empowering—up to the point when individuals abandon discrimination.

Healthy freedom advances proportionately with self-discipline to handle new freedoms. Freedom and self-discipline remain two sides of the same coin.

Psychology changed more than physics in the 20th century!

How much did psychology change between 1965-1975? Physicists lay claim to the idea that their field changed more than any other field in the movement from Newtonian physics to quantum mechanics. However a darn good case can be made that between 1890 (Freud) and 2000, psychology transformed more quantitatively and qualitatively than even physics. In some hundredth monkey phenomena, between 1968 and 1972 all progressive elements in psychology moved from

materialistic values	to	humanistic values
expert-driven	to	self-help and everyone join in
serious	to	playful but still accountable

dg7

Could this be a magnitude of change equal to or greater than in physics?

More on developmental age of the basic self

One joyful puzzle of the basic self is how to express its intelligence in terms the conscious self can work with and that provide diverse therapeutic directions. In conventional psych the idea of "mental age" exists. My take on this is mental age diverges from physical age only in exceptional cases. This is much too narrow a conception to chart or measure the intelligence of the basic self.

"Develpmental age" is an improvement int hat now we can talk more freely about adults who, for instance, with Downs syndrome, who have yet to progress past developmental age four.

A concept even more flexible is needed to describe the aspects of intelligence int eh basic self for this reason: the developmental age of the basic self has a lot to do with the agenda the soul is trying to accomplish this embodiment.

I met a woman the other night who invited me to test the age of basic self. It tested as age 3.5. This is on the young side and I wondered why such an intelligent woman had such a young b/s. Listening to her further, it made sense, a lot of sense. She needed a young child to keep her young, to keep her out of feeling old in her body. The youth of her b/s was part of her learning to have fun and joy in 3D as a soul.

The same night a second woman invited me to measure the age of her b/s. Her problem was I told her most b/ss were in the age range of 3-5 years old. When she asked the age of her b/s, she just kept counting and counting. Turned out her b/s was developmental age 15, much older than most. At around developmental age nine, the b/s is awake enuf to read energies on other people if it is directed to. Sure enuf, this woman had a very mature countenance and her goal was to be a healer of some kind. So an older, wiser b/s was vey appropriate for her soul aims in that discussion.

-=+ -=+ -=+

3S 105:

A few words on the psyche

Famous placeholder terms redefined

If your define sub-conscious as "partly conscious" and unconscious as "not at all conscious," all you've done is tell us what they are not.

Defining something by what it's not, yields only placeholder terms, words that point to unknowns. Creating such placeholder terms is dangerous because they easily become empty containers any speaker can fill with whatever they wish to place into them.

This describes much of the theoretical instability of psychology prior to the 1970s if not until the early 1990s with Bertrand Babinet. Earlier drafts of this book had long sections on how only a tiny fraction of psychological language, in the West, common in the

1800s, all the way up to WW II, survives today. Extensive reading by this author suggests far more psychology prior to 1950 has been jettisoned than has been retained. Heck, this appears true even if we move the date up to 1985. So what we call mainstream psychology today is only a recent, topmost, fertile layer with shallow roots in some respects.

It's possible to turn this sorry situation around, to begin defining the words "psyche," "subconscious," and, "unconscious" in much more precise terms; and, in terms of health, optimal wellness and wholeness. This is what's needed for 21st century psych. The 3S model offers very clear conceptions of sub- and unconscious health. It can do this because it distinguishes both a lower sub- and unconscious and a higher sub- and unconscious on either side of the rational mind:

Higher unconscious above the mind: spiritual assistance from your own high self and higher Beings

Lower subconscious above the conscious self: intuitions you hear and can act on, analogous to lower levels of the high self

Conscious, rational mind

Higher subconscious below the mind: liking and disliking in the habit body, early childhood issues.

Lower unconscious below the conscious self: metabolic

activity, breathing, blood circulation, hidden, cloaked and disguised memories, the lower level of the basic self.

The next chapter takes this further.

"Psyche" is a good placeholder term

This wonderful ancient Greek word is now best defined as

The whole of one individual human consciousness in 3D embodiment.

Dictionary.com adds, "psychological structure of a person." As a "container word," "psyche" does a good job of holding the sum of all personality factors in one individual, both factors known by the individual; and, factors unknown by the individual, but obvious to others; all of these factors.

We use psyche here to include everything in the conscious mind, sub-conscious and unconscious, both above and below the conscious self. This means psyche includes everything you know about yourself; and, everything you don't know about yourself. Whatever is present in you known and unknown that's your psyche.

We use personality here as a near synonym for psyche. To me, you are what you are, whether you know all your facets consciously or not. This truth is especially evident in a client practice. What parts of themselves clients identify with, is often a fraction of what a neutral observer sees. We are all more transparent to others than we are to ourselves! This is why we need each other to heal. This is why looking on people with eyes of love is so meaningful: We all crave to be seen thru eyes of love.

What is "behavior"?

A story serves to characterize behavior as opposed to stated intention. Once there were two sisters, Nellie and Nancy. They lived in the same house with their mother. From time to time, mother would ask, "Girls, would you help me, please?" Nellie would say, "Oh mother I was just going out to play. I love you very much. Can I come help you next time after I play? See you later." Nancy would come and assist her mother and not say a thing. Nancy learned how to bake cookies, make spaghetti, make clothes and many other interesting things.

Both Nellie and Nancy exhibit behavior. Behavior is primarily what you do; deeds vs. words.

"Spirit" and "soul" as placeholder terms

"Spirit" is only a fair placeholder term in my mind. Several different sections on soul/spirit in earlier drafts were written and removed. If anyone sees a good way to talk about spirit in the context of the 3S, I'm open to suggestions. My best attempt is: Spirit is anything invisible that you know is real. This suggests how qualities like "honesty," while invisible, are accepted as real.

The soul as defined here, is the eternal, immortal part of each person. We are asked to make sure we are cooperating with our own basic self first . Then more is added.

v\V/v

3S 106:

The invisible is
highly pattrerned & conditioned

~"~"~"~"~"~"~"~"~"~"~"~"~"~"~

We are lived by powers we only pretend to understand.

~ W.H. Auden

Your task is to gain an insight into what the human being really is ~ Rudolf Steiner (*Study of Man*, 1919) p 98.

~"~"~"~"~"~"~"~"~"~"~"~"~"~

...people sometimes prefer problems that are familiar to solutions that are not ~ Neil Postman, Co-author, *Teaching as a Subversive Art*

~"~"~"~"~"~"~"~"~"~"~"~"~"~"~

Human experience is highly patterned. Tho invisible, our psyche is highly patterned and conditioned. If people were not patterned similarly, we would be unable to understand one another. If no patterns, there would be no predictability. This would block familiarity, the pre-requisite for relationships.

What patterns--more significantly--what healthy patterns of behavior are students learning in Psych 101 classes today? Things are murky enough in conventional psychology for the cover of the March, 2001 issue of Psychology Today to ask, "What Really Works?"

How is the human psyche patterned?

Recognizing patterns is common to all sentient beings, one of the earliest expressions of intelligence, a premiere capacity of the right brain. Pattern recognition forms the foundation of many more complex and elegant forms, such as language.

You have TWELVE (12) Senses

Everyone reading this has more senses they could make

more and better use of. Why don't we have full use of all our senses? Cultural blinders put on us as children, learned thru osmosis, thru cultural conditioning, told us what to feel and how much to feel, what to see and how much to see, what to listen to and how much to listen. To the degree our cultural blinders reduce the openness of sensory channels babies come into the world with, "cultural blinders" are also "tunnel vision" imposed on our senses.

This is not bad or evil. My guess all 3D planets with people living on them have some version of shutting down a baby's senses; Earth has its own versions of this. We all agree to work within all these "myths" with particular cultural blinders, when we agree to be born here.

Q: Can you help me see these cultural blinders on my senses?

A: Easy, one key is to escape the box that your senses begin and end with only touch, taste, smell, sight and hearing. This is a 19th century Western myth. You do not have to live in it.

Q: How can I remove my cultural blinders?

A: Psychedelic drugs are one way. I don't recommend this tactic as psychoactive drugs almost always permanently distort your unconscious etheric body. This kind of damage requires very skilled practitioners to repair because the damage is all invisible.

Good sex, loving sex, feeling safe to open up more unconditionally at deeper and deeper levels, is a good way to expand your sensory channels.

The third approach is perhaps going to be more common: removing the blocks to self-sensitivity. You don't need more or better senses; you simply want to remove the chaos and incoherent aspects of the senses you already have, that you had taking your first physical breath here.

Removing the obstacles and blocks to your senses is a path of patience, gradualness and perseverance. Along the way, your inner child becomes unblocked and more free to express, so it's a good path, a happy path. Beyond that comes unblocking the senses of your Inner Court. I'm working on my blocks here myself.

Q: Which sense do I work on first? How?

A: If you can self-test, you might explore measuring your five senses, called VAKOG in NLP, on a scale of 1-10. Once you have your numbers, see what comes to mind to strengthen your weakest sense. If sensory awakening is your cup of tea, See Bernard Gunther's page at Amazon: http://www.amazon.com/Bernard-Gunther/e/B001HCZ4ZG/ref=ntt_athr_dp_pel_pop_1 He wrote the main exercise books on waking up the senses published in the early 1970s.

How we got limited to five senses

What were they thinking when Westerners limited sensing to only five senses? This happened between 1750-1850 in the West, but maybe a reader can correct me on this. Fortunately we do not have to go back and read that stuff. Rudolf Steiner (1861-1925) made a career out of braking open the overly-rigid stereotypes that cascaded into mainstream and then popular culture during the Industrial and then the Scientific Revolution in the West. He especially enjoyed busting cultural myths fast becoming dogma in the natural sciences in his time. RS's reformulations were based on Goethe's observations and scientific method; and, on RS's own practical and clairvoyant observation. Except in the area of personality typology, every Steinerism I can think of betters the myths of scientific materialism still taught in virtually every public school and college in 2011. If you can get a Waldorf education or take the Waldorf teacher training, TAKE IT. But I digress. Steiner's reformulations of basic concepts improve and expand on the more narrow concepts of observers using little more than the intellect. Steiner demonstrated how to observe with heart.

Rudolf Steiner says we have 12 senses

One of our most strikingly faulty formulations is the myth our senses begin and end with the five animal senses, only touch, taste, smell, sight and hearing. Steiner made short work of this error. Only five senses comes from the purely materialistic paradigm of human beings as merely and only Naked Apes. The five senses is supposed to prove humans have no more senses than mammals do—nothing more.

If you wish answers to what makes human *different from the animals,* you cannot stop at only five senses.

If you start from the Spirit, RS said, and work back to the human being here in 3D materiality, it's obvious and common-sensical what makes humans different from animals are many senses humans have *that animals do not.*

Below is his list of Steiner's list of 12 senses, slightly simplified and updated to reveal his most significant insight, an expansion of the kinesthetic sense beyond even how NLP conceives of "kinesthetic." See how many senses you recognize in your own awareness.

1. Sense of another soul ~ capacity to sense another person, most dramatically exercised by incidences of sensing the presence or absence of another person in complete darkness. This sense is commonly expressed in our love of socializing, parties and any peaceful groups.

2. Sense of Thought ~ the brain as a sense organ for ideas. The capacity to perceive, "I think; therefore, I am," *is an idea.* Contrast this with your sense that crying and laughing are not ideas *in that same sense.*

We perceive crying and laughing are not ideas. E = MC2, that's another idea.

3. Sense of Speech ~ capacity to make sense of speech. Even if someone is talking to you in a foreign language, you can tell if meaning is intended. Our sense of speech is heightened in viewing pantomime; we perceive meaning can be conveyed even without words.

4. Hearing audible sounds ~ this is our first sense to wake up and our last sense to leave at death.

5. Seeing colors ~ capacity to register impressions with the eye.

6. Tasting

7. Smelling

====================

The kinesthetic senses, regrouped by bd

8. Kinesthetic sense of Warmth ~ Am I warm enuf; am I too hot? Am I too cool?

9a. Kinesthetic sense of Touch

9b. Kinesthetic sense of Texture

9c. Kinesthetic sense of Weight ~ capacity to sense if something has any weight at all, capacity to sense if it has much or little physical mass, independent of size.

10. Kinesthetic sense of Balance ~ perceptions of things in or out of balance, physically, emotionally, and also morally: fairness and unfairness. Related to our vestibular sense. Highly related to intuitive hunches as in, "Something feels off here," "That sounds "funny" to me;" and, "That feels really right on target!"

11. Kinesthetic sense of Movement ~ capacity to perceive direction of movement: above to below, left to right, front to back, etc. Also our sense of relative motion, one thing in motion relative to another thing.

12. Kinesthetic sense of well-being ~ capacity to feel good, "I feel good today," "I don't feel well today;" and, I feel better today compared with yesterday."

Bruce speculates our Sense of well-being is very likely our strongest of all kinesthetic senses; as in, "I feel good today!" and, "I have a good feeling about this," and, "I have a bad feeling about this." Our poor accuracy rate in predicting future outcomes does not prove we have no such sense. Tracking when we are accurately predict good and bad outcomes is the natural starting place for further observations here.

Arranged in the above manner, human beings have SEVEN kinesthetic senses.

Any of these senses you wish to have *greater* awareness of?

Exercises:

- Rate your sensitivity on each of the 12 senses, on a scale of 1-10.

- Which one(s) would you like to "turn up the volume" on? For what purposes?

To Learn More:

The original source material in Steiner's *Study of Man* is perhaps impenetrable for most readers. This author's original work puzzling thru, piecing together and updating RS's Study of Man material for modern readers was written for an Honors Masters Thesis in college titled, *Composing Your Own Vision of Whole-Child K-12 Education*. It is available and can be emailed for $5.00 but is only of scholarly interest.

80 years of exploration and experiment, several generations of teachers internationally, have contributed to the proving of 12 senses. The 12 senses intersects with the three selves in two areas. The 12 senses supports the idea that personal experience is not primarily mental, is way beyond mere mentality. Second, if we have all these senses, the basic self has capacities undreamed of by most people. We are doing lots more than we thought we were doing in the sub-

and unconscious.

What is a percept?

Steiner agrees with the five sense folks that we receive sense impressions thru our senses. What comes thru each of our senses? Percepts. "Perception" applies to anything received from one or more senses. We often employ two or more senses at the same time without knowing. Steiner demonstrated this in his famous example of how we perceive a red circle with both our sense of color (red) and our sense of movement (roundness).

How we change lanes in traffic

Describing and defining percepts is like trying to describe and define the mind with the word "mind." That reminds me of a story. When you are driving your car in traffic, why do you change lanes? What happens to cause you to change lanes in traffic? Is it something happening inside or outside that causes you to change lanes? Naturally, you may change lanes for either something inside OR outside. We may see a car slowing or speeding up. We may recall we need to buy gas immediately. We may see a pretty girl. We may feel drunk and move to a slower lane.

Would you agree we change lanes for small "reasons?" That's what percepts are, the small "reasons" we use to make decisions. So percepts are the little things we receive thru multiple channels.

Q: But I change lanes while driving without thinking most of the time.

A: That's right. The human being has many perceptual avenues (senses) that are independent of the rational mind (sense of idea).

Perhaps this is the place to mention Steiner's observation that our percepts also come to us in three qualities of consciousness: waking, dreaming and sleeping. We may change lanes due to any percept from any of 12 senses; and, we may grasp the percept in either a waking, dreaming or sleeping state. Now you know why you change lanes sometimes and when you think about why, you are not altogether sure why you changed lanes.

A percept is a discrete impression from one of our twelve senses. Whether you know about all twelve or not, all twelve are active in all healthy persons, during all waking hours, at all ages. As RS pointed out, this has meaning for early childhood practices. With maturity and practice we learn to be more objective about our percepts. Objectivity is a primary means of discerning, verifying and validating human potentials.

We'll see in 3S 306 people typically have a preference for experiencing life perceptually (P) or conceptually (J).

Triangulating experiences thru our senses

What do we do with all these percepts? When we drag the Christmas tree into the living room to be set up on Christmas Eve, we want to make sure it's not crooked and leaning. How do we do this? We can look at the tree from one angle and see if it matches our own experience of "straightness." That uses two senses. We can also simply look at the tree from the sofa; then, walk around to the stairs and look at the tree again. That's using one sense two times.

Here's some familiar representations. They are all maps. Only maps. The map is not the territory.

Sensory representations– color, sound, weight, texture, brightness, taste smell...

Feeling sensory representations– sucking, neediness, feeling emptiness or hollow...

When we set up a Christmas tree in the living room, how do we tell if it's straight or not? We must look at it from at least two different angles, two different standpoints. This is called triangulation. Western culture trains us to triangulate outer things precisely--it trains us to triangulate inner experiences almost not at all. That's why so many Western teens feel their inner life is empty, an emotional desert. They have too little encouragement to accept their own inner experience; and, too little exposure to the idea these are all representations; and, are given too little language with which to speak about all this. The classics of Western literature and Western psychology address this, but only indirectly and anecdotally for the most part. NLP was the first set of techniques permitting people to understand and talk about how we construct--and can change--our inner lives with precision.

Representations are the meaning of meaning

Another word for "triangulate" is "represent." We represent each the experience of meeting Michelangelo's "David" statue for the first time by multiple representations: shape, color, gesture (movement), feeling that all add up to its meaning for us individually. For individuals, representations are the meaning of meaning.

This in simpler language is what triangulating experiences is. Each of our experiences is composed from multiple percepts. The representations and meaning that is stored become our memory of that experience. When we recall our memory of the "David" statue, we call forward our representation of our earlier experience, a set of remembered percepts.

This is how all experience can be representations. This is how all meaning can be subjective–for better and worse.

Pattern: All perception in 3D

is exclusively subjective

Beginning in the 1930s General Semantics began saying, personal experience is inevitably inner experience, a wisdom not seen since ancient times in the East.

In terms of what we base our choices on, there is no objective outer reality

A comprehensive objective reality is never going to be possible. Two or more persons are never going to have the same exact experience of the same object or event here in 3D.

3D Reality is necessarily, primarily subjective--because

Perception is always primarily subjective.

We can only know the external world thru our personal senses. What we call 3D reality is only our personal collection of percepts of the external world

All our percepts come thru our unique personal filters (preferences and life experience filters) each person's collection of percepts for an external object are necessarily partial and partial in a way more or less unique to that person.

THEREFORE, our experience of the 3D world is defined by the number and quality of sensory percepts and impressions we deem significant.

FURTHER, if you have no percepts or language for things I am perceiving, said things do not exist for you.

CONVERSELY, if you can gather language and percepts for things you were previously "blind" to, then said things begin to have reality for you.

What if everything ALL psychologists have ever discovered was simply called personal experience.

That simplifies matters!

Now we have one big whole, how we experience ourselves. That's the forest of psychology. Everything else is trees.

If the forest of your psychology is dark now, what's the way out?

This is the way out:

Personal and spiritual growth are becoming one thing again: Upgrading your habits and behaviors on all levels. Towards what? Towards becoming fully human and optimally healthy.

The particulars of "fully human and optimally healthy" are defined as diversely as there are diverse cultures and unique individuals.

Pattern of perception: VAKOG

The above summary of General Semantic presuppositions in the 1930s, laid the foundation for NLP in the 1980s, to come in and build a fifty room mansion..

NLP started construction on the idea that, not only do we each experience the 3D world subjectively, we experience ourselves subjectively. You don't experience me the same as I experience me and vice versa.

This is why the five outer senses of conventional nineteenth century science: taste, touch, hearing, sight and smell, are not to helpful for perceiving inner activity, doubly significant because so much of everyday language is based on outer sense percepts.

Once more people move to the viewpoint that at least half of our senses are internal, a healthy psychology of growth will leap forward.

Fortunately, NLP said, precise observation reveals which percepts a person is using to base specific behaviors upon. The percepts you use to base this or that behavior on, can be known consciously and are patterned into categories: visual, auditory, kinesthetic (VAK).

Because even young children see, hear and feel, everyone is qualified to speak--age-appropriately--on the topic of, "How do I experience myself?"

So GS is a healthy pattern: all percepts are subjective; all percepts are viewed thru subjective filters. No exceptions in the 3D experience. The spiritual corollary here is: soul is choice. Hmmm, another pattern, since all readers have souls.

Pattern: known and unknown in the psyche

What if we reduced all of psychology to just known and unknown, using white to represent known and dark representing unknown.

dg8

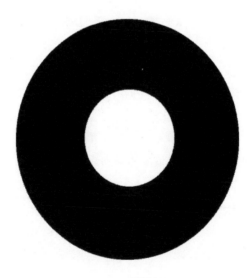

Next is a more sophisticated version. Now the inner white circle shows how the light of the known is not either or, but graduated from waking, thru dreaming to sleeping.

The central light area I call the campfire of the conscious self, our comfort zone. The further and further you go outside the campfire, the more dim our wakefulness is. Go far enuf and things are completely dark.

dg9

Of course the black, the unknown, goes on outward infinitely.

The adult conscious self is the only "light" it knows well —in the small "s" ego sense--suggesting how the c/s can feel so isolated, "like an island" unto himself.

The whole of personal experience is *both* the lighted field (white) and the larger field of unknowns around it (dark). Things close to us are lighted and visible; things far away are dark.

Fit your experience?

Note relatively little of the circle is bright white light.

The conscious self is awake to maybe 10% of its entire individual psyche.

Note how most of the circle is dim or gray, neither black nor white; suggesting, how "knowing" is so often mixed with "not knowing."

The circle is a view of the psyche from either above or from the side; suggesting, things dimly known are present to the side, above, below and all around our waking self.

The vertical scheme below suggests how we experience our waking awareness as a column of Light and how we experience the rest of our psyche from within our own light column.

dg10

The c/s lives only in the known, "lighted" area (RS)

We feel and intuit the brightly lit area of the psyche as close to us, the "me that I know." In this lighted area, we know what we like and make choices: I want a drink; put on a sweater; Amy needs a valentine; let's make one with little Jimmy after dinner dishes at 6:30 pm.

The lighted area of the "I" is where we experience our self as awake, aware and in control of our immediate external and internal environments.

The lighted area is our capacity to take hold of things consciously and know that we know them. You are reading this book. You know you are reading this book. No one can convince you that you are not reading this book. You can put the book down. You can pick up a different book and read it and you will know the difference. If you go take a bath, you will know this is different from reading a book. Pick up a pencil. You know you have a pencil in your hand. That's the lighted space of the "I."

It's possible to say, "Yes but, the pencil is made of atoms and I don't see the atoms. Therefore, I don't really know the pencil and the pencil may not exist."

This takes us away from sense percepts and into abstraction and fantasy. These have their place--but not here in psychology, the nature of becoming more fully human. Such intellectual fantasies can always be identified because they add nothing even if they are true.

The maximum knowing you can have about the pencil in your hand is present right now. Thoughts of atoms show your ability to speculate and be curious. They don't change your degree of certitude about the pencil in your hand.

A good metaphor for the soul is a column of Light. You are a column of Light. The waking "I" is portable. You can walk around, your "I" illuminating whatever is close to you, like holding a lantern. See a terrific visual of this in the very first Star Trek movie, where Vija, as a "column of light" "invades" the Enterprise and moves around the main deck, simply investigating. Things near are well lit; things far are dim or dark. As you move around, new ground, people and objects come into view, come to light. The farther away things are from the "I," the more obscure to the "I."

This is where the great value of directionality comes in. Readers will intuit that the white bar fades out both above and below the center "I." Above and below the conscious "I" things are dimmer too.

Other conscious activities in the lighted area include...

-looking for an address on an unfamiliar street,

-planning a lesson,

-planning to go to college,

-parallel parking,

-getting to the airport on time for a plane,

-writing a letter,

-cooking a soufflé,

-reading a balance sheet and budgeting money,

-using tools and heavy equipment.

All these require waking attention. You can't be dreaming or sleeping and be very effective with a power saw. We only feel in control of ourselves, in control of our life, in just those activities we undertake consciously.

Yes, we can immerse ourselves in things and places we don't understand. We can be lost. We may be making that soufflé on Mars, the first one ever made on Mars. We may feel mystery about the Martian landscape and lessened gravity. Still, we make that soufflé with our wits about us, in the lighted area of our personal consciousness, doing the best we can. That's the "I."

The lighted area travels wherever the I goes.

We may hate our mother while we make the soufflé. The hate comes in from somewhere outside the lighted zones, doesn't it? Still the hate does not make the soufflé. We make the soufflé. Thoughts of hating our mother may intrude but need not prevent us from cooking. We can overcome a little resistance.

If we did not make the soufflé consciously, if we did things primarily UNconsciously, then we could get out the ingredients, go to sleep, wake up and the soufflé would be risen and ready to eat.

The most God-like capacities of the "I," even above creative work, is our capacity to make choices, decisions and set intentions. Mistakes, poor judgment, errors are all part of the learning curve in the lighted area. That's why someone once said, "A mistake is only an error I haven't learned from yet."

The lighted area in our model is where we feel most comfortable in our personal experience. Hence the term comfort zone. When we go to sleep or take a nap, we give up awareness of the station of the conscious I.

Dim and dark regions both above and below

What about those dimmer regions above and below? All sorts of things just out of reach above and below us, to name two: Anger and resentment. Inspiration and

Kinship with All Life (1976).

In our model so far, light means known, darkness means unknown. Therefore dim means partly known. Our awareness in dim light is dull compared to the precision we have close to the conscious "I."

The curious "I" perceives things going on both ABOVE and BELOW the threshold of conscious awareness. The dim areas are all around us. The dim ABOVE seems to be qualitatively different from the dim BELOW and consistently so. We intuit dully, without understanding much (we have no language for this difference yet) that the dim above and below differ in quality.

Put the whole picture together

This might be a good time to review the very front pages where the 3S are described in single pages. These are closely written because they pack in many metaphors at once. See Therapeutic Metaphors (David Gordon, 1978) for my inspiration for this kind of writing.

In dream analysis, a very useful approach is all parts and characters stem from the "I;" all parts are aspects of the dreamer. This is true in the three selves too. All parts of the 3S are us too. We are all the players in our drama, we are all the voices, we are all the parts. Something supports the swimmer from below; something shines down helpfully on the swimmer from above. Sound like three aspects or levels of self to you?

Not four, not seven, not twelve: three.

We encounter these three levels of activity on a daily basis. For instance, we have only to shift our attention a bit to remember the "I" is supported by nutrition from "below" in the natural environment (food, mostly below us); and, by the warmth of the Sun above, who makes it possible for all plants to grow.

Our personal experience comes out this way over and over:

Higher something, waking state, lower something

We can also call them

> higher unconscious

> waking state

> lower unconscious.

We show this list vertically because verticality is part of the intuitive match: spiritual connectedness above; kinesthetic and metabolic capacities below. This intuitive match is based on the relative position of these functions relative to the human spine.

Below the swimmer, in the dim lake waters, much is going on: likes and dislikes, deeper feelings, food digestion, eye blinking, other habits and reflexes.

Above the swimmer, the Sun is brighter, even too bright to look at directly. Activity going on above is somewhat obscure to the conscious I. We are less conscious of what goes on in the level of higher inspiration and guardian beings who overshadow us, sunlike, at all times. The Sun has always represented the impersonal support we receive from spiritual beings above us.

Personal experience breaks down into these three levels over and over. A three part model covers in a general way all categories of experience people have. It's a general enough model that five billion more or less unique variations can easily exist. Everything else following is going to expand on the above three-fold model of personal experience.

We invite readers to test this model, this hypothesis, and see if it fits for them. Comments very much welcomed.

Child/human development patterns

Jean Piaget articulated the patterns of how the rational intellect emerges developmentally and comes into its own at independent thinking. Erik Erikson articulated the patterns of developmental crises everyone goes thru as they age. Steiner and Gesell articulated patterns of child development, broader than Piaget or Erikson. Steiner's and Gesell's patterns proved to be the most applicable to K-12 education. Steiner's are the only ones that made it into a system of education: Waldorf whole-child education.

The findings of Freud, Jung and a hundred other 20th century psychologists could be listed here. Each attributes to the c/s useful aspects of the human psyche. If we summarized these findings here, we would have another thick psych text, readers have hefted, felt the weight of--and set aside. Academic psych texts, God bless them, are often guilty of losing readers by describing each tree in psychology without a sense for the whole forest and what direction to move in.

Anyone who has an unresolved disturbance is like Hansel and Gretel lost in a dark forest. A tree catalog is not going to help Hansel and Gretel; even less, a catalog of tree diseases.

Growth is self-discovery

The Three Selves takes us back to these simple ideas and I wish more topics and teachers did. Humanistic Psychology grouped its studies around "growth is self-discovery." Then things went back to more mundane pursuits.

When K-12 school curricula and methods follow and match healthy child-development stages, you get the explosions of talent and joy seen successful Waldorf-methods and some charter schools.

The K-12 classroom is a wonderful laboratory for observation. Each K-12 school is a longitudinal picture of human development. The trends of both healthy and unhealthy human development is obvious in the "picture" of a child over 12 years. Consequently, models of personal experience and learning can be field tested here. Is this done? Rarely. One bottleneck is university involvement to support teachers down in the trenches who are too busy to manage research-based study. Teachers want good models of experience and learning to explain past behavior, deal with present behavior, and predict future behavior. University teacher training professors will have to take the lead— once they align with a healthy model.

Any good models in traditional education psychology?

All public school districts have licensed school psychologists, credentialed school counselors and sometimes social workers. Educational psychology is an established, respected professional field. If we want to find common language for psychology, maybe we should look here.

No disrespect to the capable and sincerely motivated professionals in this field, including the author. What we find is no serviceable model of personal experience and a gigantic gap between what is known in universities and what is practiced in conventional factory schools. William Glasser, author *of The Quality School,* (2nd ed, 1992), *The Quality Teacher* (1993), and more generally *Choice Theory: A new psychology of personal freedom* (1998), etc. provides healthy psychology to many if not most teacher trainees and counselors. But its penetration into conventional districts is slight. Hence, the rise of charter schools, new wine skins for new wine.

You can't get to being fully human and optimally healthy from analyzing how sick people are. If your child's school employs psychology based on fully human and optimally healthy, consider yourself blessed. This is very much the mood in Waldorf whole-child schools, a big reason parents support these schools.

Limitations of quantum physics for the psyche

In the 19th century, intellects wanted to find the irreducible building block of creation. Further, this irreducible building block had to be physical; or, at least completely understanding in only material-physical terms. They settled on the irreducible "block" the atom.

By the same logic they reasoned the psyche must be built up out of atoms too or at least chemicals. In the 1990s quantum scientists said the 19th century got it exactly backwards. Consciousness is the irreducible building block of creation and matter is composed of consciousness. This was indeed a step forward.

A quantum psychology has yet to develop that I know of. What is useful is the encouragement to talk about fields, that fields accompany matter and even predispose the creation of matter. Some scientists go so far as to say a field of intelligence pervades the universe--is the universe. They suggest intelligence need have no specific 3D location; it being omnipresent. This gets us closer to understanding the etheric in Creation but takes us away from our physical body, further and further into abstractions. Neither 19th century nor quantum scientists seem to be able to locate consciousness in the human being or body with useful precision. It's nice to say intelligence is everywhere, flowing around and through all beings and all processes, all things intimately connected with an infinite intelligence--but to engage Psych 101 students, let alone Energy Detectives who earn an income form assisting people to uncover and clear disturbances leading to chronic and acute disease conditions, such talk provides precious little therapeutic direction.

So far the Quantum discussion tells us nothing about the qualities of intelligence we have, making distinctions within our intelligence; nor, how these distinctions are configured. The 3S does both of these.

Nested presuppositions

Later NLP research is very fond of the topic of presuppositions. Scaling various presuppositions against each other is a matter of which of two boxes is bigger? The smaller one tends to go inside the larger one. If you have a set of nested boxes, or Russian dolls, you can move from a smaller box up to a larger; or, from a larger down to a smaller.

The largest, most expansive and inclusive platform, is most capable of embracing, sheltering and nurturing other less expansive philosophies. To use a political-religious metaphor, the largest philosophy is like a big tent, within which all can gather.

The biggest tent I can find so far in psychology is the three selves. The three selves may be a common language for psychology, a big tent.

Readers who feel some other psychological model is a more effective big tent for psychology are very welcome to make their case for it. Email me, I'm interested.

Personal experience follows patterns like everything else in creation. The three selves appears to be the larger pattern in personal experience The 3S is not a religion—just patterns and how they work. Once the pattern is clear, language becomes clearer and we can speak with each other, learn from each other

Other healthy patterns

Healthy growth pattern: From ego to empathy

A healthy growth pattern is moving from "ego" to

"empathy." Carl Rogers remains in many ways the best reference point for a psychology of empathy. Rogers went beyond New Testament psychology which says, "Do unto others as you would have them do unto you," and evolved this to, in a phrase of John-Roger, "Do unto others as they would be done by."

This is a motto of empathy. Insight into the needs of others is really called for.

Our pressing needs are to understand, have compassion, forgive and negotiate

Prior to the 1970s, psychotherapy was preoccupied with finding a formula for cure to parallel

$E = MC2$ in physics, the same old 19th century search for a single paradigm, a single unified point of view. This always pleases the intellect because then it feels more in control; defining is controlling.

Empathy has no need to control the world from a single point of view anymore than the Sun controls the planets by its light. Empathy embraces multiple paradigms and multiple points of view.

Combine intellect and empathy and we have the most powerful tool imaginable, an unparalleled problem solving tool for disturbances of all kinds.

Healthy distinction: the difference between intellect and intelligence

Joseph Chilton Pearce clarifies the difference between intellect and intelligence. Intellect is merely clever and may or may not be yoked to human values. Intelligence is always linked to the preservation and growth of the whole, for the highest good of the whole.

Sympathetic nervous system = conscious self.

Parasympathetic nervous system = basic self.

Steiner clarified this entire topic by introducing the idea (1919) that

some of our nervous system behavior is waking,

some of our nervous system behavior is dreaming, and

some of our nervous system behavior is sleeping.

Sleeping, dreaming and waking is a pattern RS found in the human psyche and physiology, for example:

dg11

Waking	thinking, choosing, deciding, initiating action
Dreaming	daydreaming, feelings in general
Sleeping	peristaltic action, eye blinking and other reflexes, cellular activity.

Nerves under our conscious control, are called the sympathetic system; they are sympathetic to the conscious self. Nerves controlling metabolic activity--activity clearly in the domain of the b/s—are sympathetic to the b/s; or, para-sympathetic. A hundred years of experimental evidence exists for this division in the topic of dowsing; and more recently, in muscle testing.

What this author suspects is that conventional physiology of the nervous system does not become elegant unless and until it rearranges its categories along the lines of one self conscious and another self less conscious. Find more on this in 3S 108: Enteric and cerebral dominance.

Meeting children at their map of the world

If the work of psychology today was done, completed, as colleges imply, how come the world is so chaotic? A real psychology ought to assist us to understand, forgive and negotiate problems. So by this measure, we do not yet have a healthy psychology.

By the same admittedly limited token, we might ask, If psychology today is so complete, how come conventional K-12 public education primarily teaches alienation from our own self and our fellow humans?

Hmmm, we have a ways to go towards healthy educational psychology too. Waldorf remains head and shoulders above the rest in my experience here and congregation of Montessori schools in recent years appears to be swinging towards Waldorf, which its more coherent theory and methods .

A healthy K-12 psychology leads adults to understand children's authentic needs and to negotiate those needs against adult needs and goals. A healthy K-12 psychology leads adults to meet children at their map of the world.

If you have no map of how a child develops to become healthy and whole, you only have your own adult map of how to meet needs and reach goals.

That's why so many adults treat infants and children as if the child was a little adult. The adults have no map of a child's world to follow. Don't feel too badly about this. History books tell us "childhood" in the modern sense, is only 150 years old as an idea. As anxious as we are today about our children in the West, we are generally doing miles better than our great-grandparents. Schools who take the inner child into account all skew towards child-centered and age-appropriate, which is what works with growing beings.

Meeting pets at their map of the world

The above on children applies equally to pets. Sometimes it is easier to see with pets. Did you ever see a pet owner yell or get angry at their pet? If the owner considers their pet an equal, are they more or less likely to speak to the pet a harsh way? This is the same error we often make with children. If we met the children at their map of the world, we would have empathy. We would know they are doing the best they can. If they knew better, they would do better. Since they did not do better they ipso facto do not know better–no matter what we think! See also more on dogs in 3S 301.

Meeting plants at their map of the world

Somewhat humorously, can you see this is also the explanation for people who have a green thumb for gardening—and—those who don't?

Other good models and hypotheses

A muscular use of Imagination, Inspiration and Intuition is called for in creating new models and hypotheses. A toy model railroad tabletop display is a model with terrain, all of it easy to see. However in psychology, "models" are maps of terrain primarily invisible.

Taken as a whole, psychology is nothing more nor less

than various models of human invisibles. How well a map fits the invisible terrain it endeavors to map, determines the value of the map. A model is a set of possibles: the terrain might be like this. Precise language is needed to be creative with invisible terrains.

Please recall how a model is related to a hypothesis in science. A hypothesis is not a definition. A hypothesis says if this...then maybe this. A hypothesis is not trying to be true or be the final answer. Once we begin to think we have the only right answer, we have caught the "holy man's disease;" that is, righteousness.

A good model becomes widespread and eventually you have a common language for people working in the same field--or tribe--or family. Common language allows explorers to share actual explorations of the new terrain. If you are a blind man groping an elephant, it helps if you all speak the same language. Otherwise you can't compare notes. So, a quality model of human experience ought to assist in our efforts to grow up and mature up.

Particular points and details may take decades to work out.

Familiar examples include Einstein's theory of relativity and the uncovery of the physical structure of DNA by Watson and Crick. Like astronomy? Most discoveries are based on models and hypotheses only later verified with telescope observations.

Another better known model is Child, Parent, Adult from Transactional Analysis. TA yielded endless two-dimensional schematics, three circles, one per self or "position." Many people responded to all this, professional and lay alike.

This book is a search for a model of the human terrain, the strongest intuitive match for the greatest number of people.

Models that don't seem to work

Hundreds of well-reasoned approaches to model the human psyche have been attempted. A longer section was removed here suggesting why several models familiar to readers, either fail to inspire young students to a life of ongoing growth and health; or, are plainly unhealthy for young minds--waters either too shallow or too deep.

Models that fail to inspire young adults can also be described as falling into two categories, models that are, on one hand, too objective and mechanical; on the other hand, models that are too subjective and amorphous, having too little rigor and intellectual precision.

Models that are too mechanical (waters too shallow)

19th century medical pathology in all its forms, forcing

strictly physical-material criteria on all phenomena of the psyche: The psyche as nothing more than electro-chemical reactions including pharmacology; and, the psyche as nothing more than genetic programming, forcing genetic explanations on all phenomena of the psyche.

Models that are too amorphous and subjective (waters too deep)

The study of auras and chakras are vastly over-emphasized in metaphysical and healing literature. Here's the problem: awareness of auras and chakras does not replace--and cannot substitute for--courage to heal, willingness to heal, making a choice to heal.

Because parapsychology studies in the 1960s, in the Us and Russia, strongly suggest each clairvoyant who can see auras and chakras sees them uniquely, these systems go farther to prove how each human being perceives uniquely. To inspire young adults and train talented sensitives, common patterns must be identified. See the New Energetic Anatomy booklet.

Etheric centers—the new term for chakras—are indeed relevant in energetic healing. The most cogent effort to create a psychology of the chakras appears to be, *Eye of the Lotus,* psychology of the chakras, Richard Jelusich, PhD. (Lotus Press, 2004).

The Goldilocks dilemma—and solution

To switch metaphors, we are left with the Goldilocks dilemma: what will nourish us cannot be too hot; cannot be too cold—it must be just right. The 3S is the only just right model of the psyche I can find. A model of the psyche able to inspire high school and college students needs to walk a middle path. It needs not to be too materialistic in its conception of the human being nor too ethereal and dissociated from the objective sense world.

.iLLi.

3S 107:

The largest pattern,

Spiritual Geography

PACME (CIEMU)

The 3S appears to be the pattern for ordering and operating a single human psyche. The 3S as a pattern exists within a larger pattern of how Consciousness is ordered. This is Spiritual geography 101, the PACME discussion.

Q: How is this relevant to the 3S?

A: The basic self is our habit body. We have habits on

all levels PACME. With awareness of where we have habits, all of which the c/s is responsible for, we are more likely to know where to look for unresolved, disturbed habits.

Much of psychology is behavior and habits. We "habitually" use habits to cope. Riding a bicycle, putting on shoes, driving a car, chewing food are only our visible habits. Only about 10% of human habits and behaviors are visible. The other 90% of our habits and behaviors are IN-visible. How we think, how we feel, how we use memories are all invisible! These invisible habits are primarily in our ACME areas.

Our habits are conditioned by preferences. Scores if not hundreds of distinct preferences are conditioning hundreds of habits we have on every level: physical, imaginative, emotional, mental and unconscious (PACME).

Spiritual geography 101

To journey on this physical level, we employ more than a physical body. It's faulty thinking that we only employ a physical body here. The physical body is only our 57 cents worth of chemical components, mostly water. The following is a technical break-out of all the "vehicles" we make use of here:

Here's the most accurate map of consciousness I've found in forty years of esoteric study. Maybe you can see it more clearly. Your comments to improve this presentation are very welcome!

The classic, modern, Western tour thru the realms can be found in Paul Twitchell's Tiger's Fang (2nd edition 2000). John-Roger shares a more personal and warm tour of the realms in When are You Coming Home? (2005).

Understanding PACME, the basic map of spiritual geography, is a good place to start, if a clear image of personal-spiritual growth is desired. It is also possible to arrange the scheme below into concentric circles. If you make it into concentric circles, the higher frequency realms become the inner circles, the outer created worlds, the lower frequencies, around them as outer circles.

The best intro to spiritual geography is experiential. In the early 1970s a certain meditation was popular and used in many learning settings. It goes like this. Close your eyes. Quiet your pictures of what you like and dislike. Now quiet your feelings about what you love and hate. Now quiet your mind. Now quiet your memories. Okay, now. Who's doing that?

The One doing the quieting–however well or poorly–is your soul, the spark of the immortal-eternal in you, in all sentient beings.

The soul is so far away from its true home here in

physical-material reality, that all we mostly see of the soul here are the qualities of loving, service, choice, friendliness, attention and intention. All the other positive qualities are more obscure, less visible down here. Hence, another blessing of the 3D experience is it highlights the most essential qualities of the soul: loving, service, choice, friendliness, attention and intention.

The soul is hard to perceive here. So it's true home might be even more obscure, right? A map can assist us.

The simple overview of spiritual geography is Mother-God and Father-God. Two regions or fields:

The Father Principle is the unchanging creaTING part.

The Mother Principle is the changing, flowing creatED part.

So Mother-Father leads to CreaTION and creaTING.

Their Son, the Holy Spirit, I think is easiest to grasp as the love, joy and synergy between Mother and Father God in their creating. So the Earth, you, me and all of creation, is their Child, their Son, part of their creation. We came out of the joy our Parents had in creating together.

So the simplest spiritual geography is a polarity.

Diagram:

Unchanging. Eternal. Stable but no fixed form. All the QUALITIES and "flavors" of consciousness-beingness.

- -

Changing. Flowing. Temporary. All the FORMS consciousness can inhabit.

These two face each other, as lovers do. The most common 3D imagery is Father God above and Mother God receiving, below. More accurately, they are interpenetrating. 3D creation is one of the final, the lowest frequency of their offspring. If they ever stopped interpenetrating, 3D atoms would stop spinning and we'd all be in trouble.

So that's the simplest map. Notice it embraces polarity, as in it takes two poles of a car battery for a car to run (John-Roger).

The next most simple map has five divisions of Mother God, of creaTION.

The simplest way to picture these five divisions of creaTION is to look at your open hand, with the thumb up. The little finger down below represents the physical level. Next finger is the level of liking, disliking, polarity and ambition (astral). The next finger represents the deeper emotions. The next finger represents the mind and beliefs. The thumb represents our unconscious memories, habits and behaviors (upper part of etheric).

There are many more words of each of these levels. Each level has its own King or God. You can read interviews with the God of each level in Paul Twitchell's book, Tiger's Fang, 2nd edition, a book justly famous for this tour of the realms. You can read a more personal account of a journey thru the realms in John-Roger's 2003 book, When Are You Coming Home?. It's very rare that anyone on Earth goes to these realms and comes back to tell about it so these two docs are really for everyone and anyone, regardless or race, creed, color or religious belief.

It's these five levels, physical, imaginative, emotional, mental and unconscious, that we deal with primarily in the human experience. Following the language of Theosophy, John-Roger calls these five Physical, Astral, Causal, Mental and Etheric. These initials spell PACME. However these Theosophical terms are from the late 1800s and have dated rapidly. More descriptive and precise terms might be: physical, imaginative, emotional, mental and unconscious. Always go for more precise language if you can get it.

Note I'm deliberately using two or more terms for the same level. If we start with multiple labels for each level of consciousness, we will start out on the correct foot: not getting hung up on labels. Each reader will then have wiggle room to define these divisions as she wishes to. Don't get hung. up on labels. What's meaningful is not the labels but the characterizations you build up in your own mind as you practice observing and thinking about the contrasting qualities of the different levels of God's body–if this pursuit appeals to you. Otherwise, just stick with the loving, make as many good choices as you can; and, forgive yourself for any choices that later seem less than optimum. That will always work.

So what's this map good for? Like any map, it's good for learning where you are now; and, to choose a direction of travel.

PACME as diagram, high frequency to low frequency

High frequency

Above soul - see Above Soul doc for some things so far learned. In general above soul are the realms of unconditioned energy--freedom--where among other things, Beings congregate voluntarily to nurture and keep alive the positive qualities of Love, Honesty, Humor, etc. Why? So these can be available in the lower frequencies of the created worlds. These qualities can only be available in the outer, more physical worlds, IF they are sustained and maintained by Spiritual Beings in higher frequencies.

-=+ -=+ -=+ -=+ -=+ -=+ -=+ -=+ -=+

Separating the unconditioned and conditioned realms, like insulation, is the Cosmic Mirror. This is where some souls coming up get stuck on the way back to soul and above. Avatars are souls who see themselves in the Cosmic Mirror and say, "I've seen God. It's me!," and give themselves the job of coming back down to save the rest of us. This action is not recommended.

-=+ -=+ -=+ -=+ -=+ -=+ -=+ -=+ -=+

Creation, the realms of the Mother-God, comprised of five levels of conditioned energy.

U

Upper etheric realm – Endlessly Fertile Womb of Creation or Zen void, depending on your emotional openness. The realm of "neither this nor that." Home of Mystery, angels, archetypes and Ur-concepts. Unconscious memories, habits and behaviors.

The Upper Etheric realm spans all of PACME and weaves the disparate aspects of different density together into wholes. The Etheric has rightly been called the "Web of Life" as it gives sentient beings the sense of being one whole rather than disconnected parts.

See also the "Lower etheric realm", below, just above the physical.

The realms below the Upper etheric can be pictured as

bands of liquid in a clear glass beaker. They form into bands according to their respective density, densest layer on the bottom. The Upper Etheric density runs thru all of them uniting them all.

- -

M

Mental realm – Form and structure. Beliefs. Mentalizing. Monkey mind. Beliefs. Allegiances.

- -

E

Emotional realm – Attachment. Deep emotion. Ten times stronger than any other realm in Creation at this time. Emotional love. Hatred. The emotions you are attached to. Attachment in all its forms, especially emotional. Called the "causal realm" in times past because attachment was seen as the cause of our karma, which is largely accurate—but not very helpful.

- -

I

Imaginal realm – Liking and disliking (see RS 1919 on this). Reactivity. Monkey mind. The more obvious five senses (animal senses). Fleeting feelings. Animal "passions." Imagination. The "blueprints" of your optimum physical body can be found here. The theosophical term was "astral realm." Astral means starry. Early clairvoyants were very impressed with the sparkly and colorful quality of the human aura and the appearance of dis-incarnate beings living on this level, who appear sparkly and colorful. New language is more appropriate for purposes of growth. Also: Pan(?), devas and nature spirits. UFOs, aliens, "Star Trek" and Federation of Planets activity.

- -

-

e

Lower etheric realm. These are the levels behind and responsible for physical vitality. This is the home of the four elements, the five elements, acupuncture meridians and all phenomena related to them. Chi! Prana! Orgone! Nature spirits. Without this level of life energy animating the physical body, all we have is a corpse. The astral frequencies are too high frequency for the physical body to assimilate. The lower etheric realm is not separate from the upper Etheric. They are a continuum, the energetic "glue" holding the whole of creation together.

- -

P

P for physical or C for Chemical or Cellular. The chemical-cellular corpse of the human being. Nothing is technically alive if we consider only the physical. Material building blocks. Things. Rocks. Rocks and plants do have living elements but these rest above the physical.

Low frequency

"Where am I on this map?"

At the mall, if you are lost, you find a big map and look for the "you are here" marker. Where's the "you are here" marker in spiritual geography? To find out where you are, ask the question, where do I spend the majority of my attention, primarily? A more precise version of this question might be, "Where is my spiritual center of gravity?"

You have a physical body yet it's unlikely your spiritual center of gravity lies in materiality. This would only be true if your whole life and everything you do is centered around things providing you comfort and pleasure for your physical body. If that were true for you, you'd be unlikely to be reading this now.

If you wish to experiment, give yourself time to consider

each level of consciousness. Which level, PACME, might represent where your center of gravity is? It is possible to have your center of gravity in the soul realms above the unconscious. Sure. It's more rare though.

The above five-fold map is often called PACME in honor of John-Roger, who did more than anyone else in the last 100 years to promote this basic orientation in the West.

To my brother and sister metaphysical bookworms, yes, you do find similar spiritual geographies in Rudolf Steiner, Max Heindel, Buddhism and many other places. All of these date from the last part of the 1800s. These other map-models are striking in that most stop at or before the Causal realm. Many older maps are complicated by Buddhist terminology difficult to translate and penetrate with Western sensibilities. The Buddhist maps may or may not cover as much territory as the PACMES model, hard to tell. Historically the Light & Sound groups have had the most clear and complete spiritual geography going.

Ultimately, all of this is only maps. Find people who love and support you and whom you can love and support.

Many, many people will not like the idea that maps of consciousness even exist. That's fine. These maps are not for those people! A map is only useful if you wish to learn where you are and to make choices about where to go. A map does not make choices for you–tho it may make some choices obvious. That's why the people who DO like maps, like them. They are helpful--but as NLP says: maps are not the territory. Don't get caught in the map!

-=+ -=+ -=+

Is every BODY happy?!

We have bodies on each level of God's Creation, physical, pre-physical (lower etheric), imaginal, emotional, mental, unconscious.

Physical: Solids, liquids and gases only.

Pre-physical: Energetic levels: Warmth; chemical-tone-interaction; light; life-- the bodies of formative forces, most familiar as acupuncture meridians, prana, chi: vitality.

Imaginative: Personal likes and dislikes.

Emotional: Deeper desires, commitments and attachments.

Mental: Concepts, beliefs, allegiances.

Unconscious: Archetypes, identifications and memories

on all levels.

The basic self maintains the integrity of all the above bodies, physical and subtle. The b/s is etheric and the etheric is connectivity. It coordinates all our bodies in accord with what we are creating--for good or ill. So one definition of the basic self is the one who holds up, supports, enables the spiritual being we are to be active here in a dense physical realm.

The b/s is in charge of the etheric centers. If it does not trust what's coming in, it will not open to those energies. So the b/s is the starting place for all dowsing and muscle testing. Any time you are dowsing or muscle testing, you are connecting outside the isolated conscious self, to other beings, thru the basic self.

Q: What about our eternal immortal soul?

A: The above bodies are all highly conditioned. The soul is not conditioned. The term "soul body" is a turn of phrase, not to equate the soul with our other conditioned bodies. Our bodies acquire conditioning by prior experience, our genetic inheritances, local circumstance and local environment. The soul is not conditioned by any of these tho it can identify with these mistakenly. Soul is beingness here to learn it is that and only that.

v/V/v

3S 108:

ENS-CNS dominance:

Do you have more

thoughts or more feelings?

Virtually every Psychology 101 textbook, starts with brain anatomy. We can well ask, "Why is this?" since most aspects of the human psyche are strikingly Invisible such as kindness, honesty, integrity, cooperation, intelligence.

Prior to the 1800s, churches outlawed anatomical dissection of human beings. When this changed and human anatomy was new, young adults were excited. What had previously been forbidden was now legal to study. It was exciting to examine brain parts! The impulse to begin study of the psyche with a study of corpse anatomy has been carried over in virtually all conventional Psych 101 textbooks to the present day.

But the young are not buying it. Human anatomy is no longer news.

HealingToolbox.org

What do they want? Young adults want hands-on experience and practical guidance, specifically to:

- Learn about ourselves. It's age-appropriate to be self-absorbed as a teen.

- Learn about people around us: family, friends, teachers. Now that I CAN understand people in my world, HOW do I understand them?

- Capture a vision of creating lifelong personal and intrapersonal health.

Q: Do we then throw out all anatomy from the Psych 101 texts?

A: No. For young adults, the contrasting anatomies of our enteric and cerebral nervous systems is a good place to begin study of the human psyche as whole.

Sympathetic and parasympathetic

In discussing two nervous system, many readers will already have been exposed to the terms sympathetic and parasympathetic nervous systems. In this older idea, the rational mind is not part of ANY nervous system and has in addition to itself two helper nervous systems, more or less intertwined, difficult to separate, each with a few distinct qualities; but for the most part, converged in one homogenous whole. My guess is this idea dates from the late 1800s. Around 1907 thru anatomical dissection in the U.S., in research preserved by the Meridian Institute, a now-defunct Edgar Cayce org, the new idea was born that the two nervous systems are anatomically distinct and not of one piece. Converge this with the three selves model introduced to the West in 1948 and you get the idea that the rational mind IS, inhabits the cerebral NS and the inner child IS, it inhabits the gut brain. This simpler idea of two distinct NSs replaces the older, more confusing terms: sympathetic and parasympathetic.

Anatomically what do we have? We have two concentrations of nerve tissues in our body. We have nerve tissues concentrated in the brain and spinal nerves. We also have, bounded above by the diaphragm muscle, nerve tissue much less concentrated, very much diffused, with nerve tissue present in many organs, most notably the omentum, the flap of nerve tissue overhanging the stomach, the location of the feeling of "butterflies in the stomach." The two areas of nerve tissue, the two contrasting concentrations of nerve tissue, should be viewed as differently as we view the rational mind and the operating system for the body, they are majorly different and distinct.

Your "gut brain" is your enteric nervous system (ENS). You also see this termed the "mesenteric nervous system;" and, "abdominal brain" in medical literature.

Your "head brain" is your cerebral nervous system

(CNS). It too is composed of nerve tissue, located primarily in your spinal cord, brain and the nerves radiating out from the spine.

Gut brain anatomy - detail

Nerve tissues in the enteric nervous system (ENS) is more diffuse than in the CNS. Nerve tissue is distributed in several organs: omentum, stomach, pancreas, spleen, esophagus and parts of the small intestine and large intestine.

The omentum is a flap of nerve tissues overhanging the stomach in front. This is the biggest quantity of nerve tissue in the ENS. This is where we feel "butterflies in the stomach," feel, "punched in the gut," and "know it in the gut," "gut instinct." These familiar phenomena are not stomach phenomena, as commonly thought.

The omentum is close to the front surface of the body and is the most conscious of our organs charged with receptivity. Keep in mind, the most conscious of these organs still remains SUBconscious.

Stomach is the next deepest organ. Its response is difficult to distinguish from the omentum as the omentum covers the stomach and has much more nerve tissue then the stomach does. Older literature lumps stomach and omentum together and with some justification.

The duodenum assists with the transition of food from the stomach to the small intestine. It does some of the "thinking" for the stomach.

Pancreas is the next deepest organ of receptivity. It's issues are difficult to distinguish from the spleen. The psychology of both organs is represented by the Earth element in acupuncture, the qualities of sympathy, emotional warmth and "sweetness of life." See a full exposition of spleen and pancreas in this author's Meridian Metaphors, Psychology of the Meridians and Major Organs.

Spleen is the deepest and most receptive and sensitive to energetics, closest to the cosmic, to receiving prana, and to being cosmic.

The nerve tissue of the esophagus is also part of the ENS.

Cerebral brain anatomy - detail

Pictures of the extent of the CNS can be seen in conventional pictures of the nervous system, especially in the topic of chiropractic: brain, nerves and the nerves radiating out from the spine.

In other words, what we used to call "my nervous system" is only one of the two, only the cerebral system; really, only half of the nerve tissues in our body.

Maryann Castellanos & HealthyEnergetics.net

I am very grateful to Maryann for raising the topic of our two nervous systems in my education. What follows below is in large part things learned from Maryann's Choice Point classes. These classes assist to flesh out the practical use of the two nervous systems. The following is an outline of her topic coupled with insights gathered at my end.

ENS & CNS are teammates

Q: Which nervous system is better, which is bigger?

A: Neither! Each nervous systems has very close to equal an equal amount of nerve tissue by actual weight; the amount of nerve tissue in the CNS above, is equaled by the amount of nerve tissue in the ENS below.

By actual weight, these two nervous systems have the same amount of nervous tissue.

You have two spines

The cerebral NS has its spine in the bony spinal cord and vertebrae.

Your second spine is softer and in front of the bony spine. The second spine is our esophagus, your throat lining going down to the stomach and your tongue.

Q: What does all this mean?

A: The ENS is a physiology of the basic self, of the repetitive, linear, sequential kind of thinking the basic self is good at and likes to do. The gastro-intestinal tract is in some ways a clear out-picturing of the kind of "thinking" going on in our sub- and unconscious.

The CNS is a physiology of the conscious self, of waking cognition, of the clear "light of day" thinking (Rudolf Steiner) in our psyche.

Note the quality of each. The physiology of the cerebral nervous system has the qualities of clarity, rays of light, directness and penetration, a sharp, penetrating "edge."

The physiology of the enteric nervous system has the qualities of warmth, roundness, patience, nourishment, gradualness, and support, its edge is dull; and indeed, "blind" compared with the CNS. The ENS operates on blind faith and touch, which are also powerful.

You have two minds

Your ENS is your feeling mind. Your CNS is your thinking mind.

Q: So what if I have two minds?

A: Do you recognize you already use one of your minds more than the other? You do not use both of them equally.

Which mind do you prefer using? You prefer to use ONE. No one I have met or heard of is exactly 50-50.

Which mind you prefer using determines how you prefer to respond to life situations. The ideal is for your feeling and thinking minds to work together as a team, each contributing their point of view to making decisions.

Consider the older language of "mental and emotional bodies." While this remains correct clairvoyantly speaking, CNS and ENS updates this old abstraction into anatomical detail and an image of healthy partnership.

The educator John-Roger takes this further: "Match a thought to every feeling and a feeling to every thought"

Matching feelings and thoughts coherently and congruently creates integration and manifests coherence in a person.

Readers familiar with Compassionate Communication (NVC) will recognize when skillfully conducted, NVC does exactly this: helps people match thoughts to unspoken feelings and encourages matching strong feeling to appropriate language.

Q: Don't we do this already?

A: Mostly no; most of us are caught up in denial of thoughts, feelings or both, from family of origin patterns. You can hear instructive examples of what matched up thoughts and feelings sound like on the NVC videos on YouTube.

Q: WHY don't we match thoughts and feelings already?

A: Safety. Our family of origin trains us in what is safe to do, feel and think--and what is not. In some families it is safe to express feelings first, less safe to match feelings to them.

In other families, thinking is preferred. It's safe to share your thoughts but not your feelings. Consequently:

An enteric dominant person

feels first and thinks second.

A cerebral dominant person

thinks first and feels second.

One way to discern your preference is by asking: Which do I have more of today, more thoughts or more feelings?

We'll give you more ways to determine your own preference further down.

Q: Can I change?

A: Yes. Change will be in terms of integrating thoughts and feelings so you can use either or both flexibly. You want a working partnership of your two minds.

Let's address any confusion between your two minds, thinking and feeling; and, your two brain hemispheres, right and left. These two concepts overlap but are not equal. The differing character of right and left hemispheres is taken up at length in *The Inner Court, Close-up of the Habit Body* at section 600, in connection with personality typology.

CNS & ENS in art: Puch & Judy, Topdog and underdog

The archetypal and artistic power of the original Punch & Judy puppet shows can be seen at the very start of Franco Zeffirelli's Romeo and Juliet, where a historically accurate Punch & Judy puppet show is enacted.

Punch & Judy is little performed today; or maybe, performed in every sitcom you can name and perhaps therefore invisible.

Modern language for Punch & Judy can be found in talk therapy int eh topic of "victim & perpetrator." It can also be found in the topic of "top dog & underdog" in Gestalt Therapy.

The therapy perspective makes clear how Punch & Judy shows out-picture what is going on in most unresolved inner conflicts.

If Punch & Judy is unfamiliar to you in any way, just imagine Mr. Spock from Star Trek in the same small room as Homer Simpson. Imagine further these two are sharing the same body and have to get along. If you can imagine these two fighting, then you understand Punch & Judy.

Gestalt Therapy points out top dog-underdog conflicts are in the vertical plane. Topdog & underdog conflicts are indeed classically between the conscious self above and the basic self below.

Dominance, preferences, & MBTI linkage

Which hand do you use first?

If you cannot experience whether you are ENS dominant or CNS dominant, we need to grasp more of what preference and dominance signify. These are major concepts in the three selves.

Preference is easy to understand. In the study of handedness, right and left handedness, the word "preference" is always used. Preference connotes something conditioned while preserving a degree of choice. Using either your right or left hand is a preference learned in childhood; a preference for either hand will work for you.

The Educational Kinesiology people and Extra Lesson people are very interested in whether a person is cross-dominant.

Cross-dominant means the person prefers using, for example, their right hand but their left foot; their right eye but their left ear. The more consistent your preferences for how you use your body and take in information, the less learning disorders you are likely to have.

Dominance is probably less well understood. "Dominant sexual characteristics" is perhaps our most familiar phrase with dominance in it. Dominance connotes two modes, such a male and female. It also has less connotation of choice than preference.

Whether you are ENS dominant or CNS dominant is in part culturally determined, based on family of origin conditioning (Behind this is the insight that E or C dominance is not so much learned in your family of origin as reinforced there. The preference we have for either E or C is so deep, it is primarily conditioned from prior existences). Enteric or cerebral dominance is so deeply unconscious, it is similar to whether we identify with being male or female. The average person accepts the one gender or the other. Same with ENS-CNS dominance.

For growth, we do have choice about our E or C dominance. The choice is either: to remain at our present percentage of relative use of each; or, choose to increase the balance more towards 50-50.

(Aside for readers who enjoy metaphysics: During the era of metaphysics (1880-1955) several mystics placed the time of the Garden of Eden in the later Lemurian period. Lemuria was the era of human evolution when the differentiation of the sexes took place. At the start of Lemuria the human being was androgynous, both male and female. A differentiation of creative forces within each individual human body took place. Human creative energy began to differentiate, half being used to generate the human physical form and organs. We now call this our metabolic forces. The other half of human creativity began to direct itself to build the nervous system, brain and larynx, towards later independent thinking. Ideally the two creative systems stay in communication and stay in balance.

Maryann Castellanos' insight is, if an individual can acknowledge their dominance pattern, this is a huge key to understanding virtually all our physical illnesses and many of our unresolved issues.

Significance of ENS-CNS dominance in a nutshell

Maryann says the short version is enterics feel first and then think second; cerebrals think first and feel second.

The significance of ENS-CNS dominance can be grasped by noting that up to now, precise language for locating and distinguishing the thinking mind and feeling mind, in the body, has been vague to none.

Once you can distinguish and locate them, you are halfway towards working with them towards wellness.

Another study might suggest the conventional language of sympathetic and para-sympathetic nervous systems led us away from grasping the more obvious and useful concept of how our thinking mind and feeling mind show up in our bodies. The language about mind and emotions in psychology need no longer be a language of separation any longer.

Enteric-cerebral balance embodies and puts flesh and bone--literally--on John-Roger's idea of matching a thought for every feeling and a feeling for every thought. ENS-CNS points to what we have to work with and how to do this.

Precise distinctions between the mind and emotions are even more vague in metaphysics and spiritual topics, either limited to discussion of "mental and emotional bodies" limited to clairvoyant perception; or, to receiving massage. ENS-CNS updates the old abstractions of "mental and emotional bodies" into an image of how to move towards balance.

Q: Why can't I find enteric-cerebral in my psychology

textbooks?

A: Maryann says that since the medical research in the 1980s on the enteric nervous system (ENS) and "mesenteric brain" that responsible scientists have acknowledged we have not one concentration of brain tissue, but two, one in the gut and one in the head.

Their dilemma is no one has made the news sexy enuf to motivate anyone to re-write the textbooks to reflect this big change. Who wants to retool a whole medical and psychiatric mechanism for the sake of mere truth? Conventional doctors trained only in the body, not in nutrition or counseling tend to say, "What difference will it make anyway?"

Q: Who can make practical use of "we have two minds"?

A: Healers, coaches and counselors unafraid to address at least etheric issues. People with problems want answers. Many of our most pressing personal problems are "hidden" by lack of practical language for etheric and spiritual topics and phenomena in the human psyche. With ENS-CNS and the 3S we can discuss psychic activity, even "hidden" activity, with much more precision and often with physiological precision.

Breathing patterns suggest ENS-CNS dominance

Q: How do I determine what my dominance is?

A: I'm glad you asked! What parts of your body do you use to breathe?

If you change your breathing as soon as you notice it, you are probably cerebral dominant. If more of your breathing MOVEMENT happens below the diaphragm belly breathing--you are enteric dominant. If more of your breathing happens above the diaphragm, in the front or sides of the chest, cerebral. The less your belly moves, the more cerebral dominant you are.

Maryann observes most everyone prefers to do their breathing either above or below their diaphragm. Chest or belly breathing dominates in a person not both. Virtually no one is 50% a belly breather and 50% a chest breather; tho, this would be healthy. In everyone one breathing dominates naturally.

This idea contradicts most breathing lore which suggests breathing fully in both belly and chest is easy to learn. ENS-CNS dominance suggests why it is virtually impossible for an individual to change their breathing pattern and maintain both belly and chest breathing, full breathing for any length of time.

Belly breathers -> Enteric nervous system dominates

Chest breathers -> Cerebral nervous system dominates

Fast & slow in the body

Do you like to travel fast or slow in your body?

Thinking with the ENS is a slower, more leisurely, more sensual, and more feeling experience. It can be very imaginative in these things.

Thinking with the CNS is a faster, more dynamic, less leisurely, more abstract, and more cognitive experience. It can be very imaginative in these things.

For enterics, thinking with the neo-cortex feels too fast, abstract and foreign. "I'm out of my element."

For Cerebrals, thinking with the gut feels too slow, too obvious, too simple and foreign. "I'm out of my element."

The enteric dominant person has easy access to "gut feelings." For them thinking objectively and abstractly is less natural.

The cerebral dominant person has easy access to abstract thinking. For them, feeling with their gut is less natural.

Caution on typing your friends

It's very tempting here to paint ENS-CNS dominance black and white and jump to conclusions about people,

"She's a this; he's a that." Maryann says this is going too far. Working out the correct dominance for an individual requires close observation. For instance, Bruce, the present author is clearly a Cerebral-dominant yet he is also a belly breather. So while patterns and generalizations exist, individual uniqueness trumps them.

More broadly, NVC has figured out language for the occasional horror stories that emerged when NLP and MBTI were brought into the corporate training world. If you use NVC, NLP, MBTI, astrology or ANY personality typing, as a strategy to manipulate people—they will feel that and back off. You are much smarter if you ONLY use these powerful tools as strategies to *connect* with another person. If you are using these tools for any other intention other than connecting, you can easily be perceived as using them to manipulate people.

E&C in a single person mix and match in more combinations than are convenient. Determining a person's ENS-CNS dominance is another art form to practice.

ENS and CNS do not blend;

they are partners

Maryann is not for blending E&C into one homogeneous system. E & C need to remain distinct, function independently. She says the two nervous systems need to be distinct as they process different parts of our 3D life here. The sympathetic NS, aligned with the c/s, is our capacity to be alert and focused. Our para-sympathetic NS, aligned with out b/s, is our capacity to relax. We want both functioning optimally.

Teamwork and differing perspectives are good here. The more you can switch back and forth between the two, the more we have flexibility.

The Honeymooners and The Flintstones

"The Honeymooners" and "The Flintstones" are the strongest displays of the ENS-CNS polarity we have come up with yet in pop culture.

The humor and drama of the Honeymooners, between Ralph Kramdon (Jackie Gleason, the enteric) and Ed Norton (Art Carney, the cerebral), make clear the dramatic, potentially explosive differences between enterics and cerebrals. They have nearly opposite ways of viewing certain things--hence the comedy.

A generation later, The Flintstones, Fred and Barney, were based on the Honeymooners characters, Ralph Kramdon and Ed Norton. Both Honeymooners and Flintstones are classic pairs of enterics & cerebrals in mutual dependence. Ralph Kramden and Fred Flintstone are the enteric. Ed Norton and Barney are the cerebrals.

Lou Abbot (the cerebral straight man) & Bud Costello (the enteric funny man-child) are perhaps the most clear enteric cerebral couple, depending on each other to be one whole person.

George Burns (the cerebral straight man) and Gracie Allen (the enteric funny child-woman) also follow this polarity.

If you have seen any of the above you also understand how dated the behavior appears. People do not act in such limited ways any more; it can even be difficult to relate to why it was funny then (Laurel & Hardy, Chaplin and Keaton have all dated much less, a credit to their genius).

This dating effect has wisdom in too. What is it precisely that's dated? It's how polarized the expressions of enteric and cerebral are in these characters. "Never the twain shall meet" in those comedies.

That we today feel repulsed by the extreme polarization between enteric and cerebral styles, evidences some collective progress in harmonizing the gap between our two nervous systems. We--collectively--are more integrated today than our grandparents generation was. That's good. It's even evolution.

You have two hands

Would you rather have just one hand or two? We can agree one hand is good; two hands are better.

ENS & CNS respond differently to stress

Maryann shares her observations of how enterics and cerebrals process the shocks, blows and traumas of life different. Her ideas throw light on how people respond to stress, based on their ENS-CNS dominance.

Let's start from a healthy 50-50 balance. We can use Compassionate Communication (cNVC.org) as "healthy natural," where matching thoughts to feelings and feelings to thoughts, are both equally safe, a goal I aspire to. We want to use "health" as the norm.

The characteristic dilemma of enterics, predisposed to the feeling mind, is to stop feeling safe to rise up and match their feelings with their thoughts.

Cerebrals, predisposed to the thinking mind, respond to stress by stop feeling safe to slow down, relax, enjoy the water, and allow their thoughts to find feelings and intuitions to match.

In more extreme situations, Maryann says enterics easily become scared out of their wits, frozen, "deer in the headlights." Enterics withdraw from the CNS, shift their energy down lower, defensibly, into their metabolic processes, in an effort to "hide" from the real or imagined severe judgments coming from above--the cerebral NS.

Bruce speculates if this pattern, starts in childhood and continues steadily, may correlate with the observed phenomena of persons with very short necks, who appear scrunched down into their physical bodies.

Not everyone is "scared out of their wits." Cerebrals easily become scared out of their feelings. More literally, scared out of their blood/digestion/ metabolic processes. This pushing the eject button and leaving the enteric NS behind articulates the mechanism of the "ivory tower" pattern in intellectuals, where cerebrals live in a secluded, narrow, high space, unable or unwilling to descend back to ground level.

Cerebrals are "scared up into their wits." No one volunteers to live their life compulsively in their head. People don't live in an ivory castle for years because the view is nice. Sleeping Beauty does not go up into the ivory tower voluntarily. She is coerced to go up there. For most people this happens thru traumatic experiences. These experiences can be PTSD from this or from prior lives. Yes, it's curable too, but it does take time and patience.

In a loving, supportive environment, examining these shocks, with or without a compatible counselor or coach, is one of the most valuable things we can do here on Earth.

Bruce speculates the ivory tower pattern, started in childhood and continued for ten, 20 years, correlates with observations made in body-centered psychotherapy, about persons with very long necks, especially tall persons, who appear stretched out vertically, up and away from the ground. The present author exhibits this pattern and is making wonderful progress to moderate and heal it.

What frustrates you?

Cerebrals enjoy closure and completion on things begun. They become frustrated when external things don't reach completion or don't go their way towards completion. Things going out of control outside themselves bother them. Control of their internal environment is less of a problem. They can be over-controlled by others and not notice it as a problem for them.

Enterics enjoy spontaneity and excitement. They become frustrated when they can't control their own inner environment. When an absence of internal control occurs, they get unhappy. Control of the external environment seems more remote and impossible to them and less of an issue.

Characteristic dilemmas of Enterics

More paraphrases from Maryann: When enteric dominants are stuck, they express as self-centered and harsh to their own basic self:" "I'm no good; I'm a failure; what's the use." The stuck Enteric feels blamey and confused, like there is no place to begin to sort things out.

When overwhelmed, Enterics repress their thinking mind. They don't want to go up and think about anything that leads to an unavoidable unwelcome judgment [closure]. Unwelcome thoughts are easy for Enterics to put aside. They like their comfortable routines and habits. These are enuf for them.

Many hard working Enterics keep themselves busy to stay out of their own truth because sometimes truth can be unpleasant. They don't feel ready for some of the truths their cerebral thinking would provide them with if they were they to go inside and "listen."

When flustered, enterics will often jump out to help others to numb their own sense of helplessness. They go out to others to stay unconscious of their issues.

Enterics have a difficult time chunking down tasks into bite-size pieces. Consequently they are very liable to feeling overwhelmed, lost and confused.

If the Enteric also expects that all those tasks have to be done perfectly, then the Enteric may simply give up and do nothing.

To get in balance, the enteric has to rise up

Maryann says the enteric has to rise up, literally, into their own neck, head and shoulders and tolerate more truth in their beingness. Enterics typically have to come up out of the day-to-day lives of their children, family and friends, come back into themselves and be less converged with other people. They need to assert their own needs more, stop being so influenced by others. For instance they may need to serve others less so they can serve their own Self more.

"In my work, if the enteric nervous system shows up for working on, this suggests the person is unbalanced. Specifically they are having trouble connecting to their own Divinity and from there, back down into themselves. They feel incapable of accomplishing things and don't know how to express love, peace and beauty back to themselves to create a safe and rich inward life. Rather than expressing their True self, they act out of somebody's idea of who they "should be," usually someone else's idea of who they should be.

"Enterics relate "own self" to "own self." They are "self-referential" in an emotional sense. The roles, images, and conditioning imposed on them by others (willingly or not) keep them from radiating their love more freely. Enterics have to overcome paralyzed thinking, come out of over-creating in the emotions and imagination. They need to learn to play by the rules of the game of incarnated life, and how to take care of themselves first.

"Enterics live in a land that is less structured than the world a cerebral creates around them self. The more an enteric is polarized towards enteric strategies, the less they want to structure. The focus stays fuzzy; and, they regard that as a good thing.

"However an overly-polarized strategy eventually has restricting and limiting consequences on your self-care. Healthy use of their thinking mind would clear up the fuzziness; but then, they would feel ashamed, have to feel the shame of looking to others for their value and not caring adequately and sufficiently for themselves. There can be outrage under that when they finally realize that there is only them in their world."

Characteristic dilemmas of Cerebrals

We can adapt the above to cerebrals:

When cerebral dominants are stuck, they express as self-centered and harsh to other people, especially the basic selves of other people. Blaming is popular: "It's your fault." Labeling is popular: "You're a louse. You're no good." The stuck Cerebral feels angry and confused, like there is no place to begin to sort things out.

When overwhelmed, Cerebrals repress their feeling mind. They don't want to slow down and feel the strong emotions boiling up inside them because they don't know what to do with them. They may have no strategies for this. Unwelcome feelings are easy for Cerebrals to push aside. They like what they like.

Many hard working Cerebrals keep themselves busy to stay out of the truth of their own feelings because sometimes truth can be unpleasant. Sometimes there is grieving and sadness to acknowledge. They fear the grieving and sadness will be infinite, unending. "Why bother starting on that? There's never an end to it." They don't realize each strong feeling has an arc and is not endless; it has a beginning, middle and end and will resolve itself if given half a chance. Also they do not realize this: You don't have to know; you only have to ask" (Maryann). The end point does not have to be known ahead of time. Healing is a process not a destination, goal or ending. This is what cerebral dominant persons who are stuck often have not learned.

When flustered, Cerebrals will often jump back, into an introverted stance emotionally. Some Cerebrals are so good at withdrawing emotionally, while appearing outwardly unchanged, they may not even know they have switched their feeling mind off. This corresponds to Virginia Satir's caricature of the "Computer" type of person, which reminds me of some engineering professionals I have met. They go away from others to stay unconscious of their issues.

Cerebrals have difficulty stepping back from analyzing and get back to the big picture that includes people's feelings. To get in balance, the

Cerebrals have to slow down, learn patience and gradualness

The Cerebral has to invest time, money, space and time to sink down into--whatever is present in the feelings, sub- and unconscious. There is truth in the lower parts of the psyche as well as unresolved disturbances to address, extract learning from and release.

Cerebrals typically have to come down into the day-to-day lives of their children, family and friends, come back into the feelings and needs they and other people have and be less concerned with what it all means. They need to listen to other people's needs more and stop being so one-sided in their thinking. For instance they may need to serve others more as a way for them to discover more of their own Self.

Cerebrals live in a land much more structured, purposeful and strategic than the world an Enteric creates around them self. The more a Cerebral is polarized around cerebral strategies, the more confident they are in the structured routines they have set up. Even when others see this as rigid, the Cerebral may see their structures as crisp, clear and working just fine.

An Enteric theme song

I listen for songs expressing the point of view of different aspects of the psyche. The Enteric theme song might be, "Green Summertime" by Robin & Linda Williams, Jerome Clark, on the album Devil of a Dream. This song was made famous on Prairie Home Companion. Excerpt:

Far off in the by-and-by
I see a traveler in the sky.
But my dreams do not take wings
For I'm captive to familiar things.
In this world of mine
In the green, green summertime
BRIDGE:
Though I know them all too well
And I have heard all they have to tell
My steps will always walk this ground
To these old friends I am bound.
© Robin & Linda Williams, Jerome Clark.
This speaks to the joys and dilemmas of the enteric.

A Cerebral theme song

The early Simon and Garfunkel hit song "I am a rock (I am an island)" sums up the dilemma of the cerebral.

Maryann says, frankly, it's all the same in the end game. Whichever way we choose to polarize in our strategy to combat stress, the result is there is difficulty standing up on our own, in the midst of pain, and allowing it to process to completion. Opportunity for trauma is all around us, so we all get plenty of practice in our strategies to deal with stress and pain. Because we are so unconscious of this mechanism, the pain happens, and our stress strategy kicks in. We polarize towards E or C a bit more.

Therapeutic indications: getting back in balance

"If you see a balanced person, they are like a balanced yin-yang symbol. They can access either polarity easily." When she herself is out of balance, to get back into balance, Maryann exaggerates her less dominant polarity. She exaggerates it to get it up to 50%, back into 50-50 balance.

The classic technique to do this with exaggerated breathing, either exaggerate chest and shoulder breathing to stimulate the cerebral nervous system; or, more commonly exaggerated belly breathing to stimulate the enteric NS.

Maryann agrees with conventional wisdom on breathwork that chest (top) breathers benefit from more bottom breathing and vice versa. She suggests the following visualizations to work with for exercising your non-dominant capacity.

For cerebral folks, imagine your head energy melting and dripping down into your belly.

For belly breathers, imagine yourself looking up to a

beautiful crown on top of your head. Imagine your arms reaching up to touch it and honor it.

If all else fails, Maryann says the best way to get out of stuckness, back into balance, is to take care of yourself. This will automatically take you towards better balance.

ENS-CNS meet and overlap in the heart

The ENS and CNS share the heart in overlapping Venn diagram fashion:

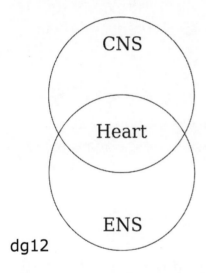

dg12

The b/s and c/s overlap in the heart center. Over time, thru the process of personal-spiritual growing (clearing unresolved disturbances), the overlap between the b/s and c/s expands. In highly evolved mystics, who have necessarily undergone years of such processing, the overlap looks like this:

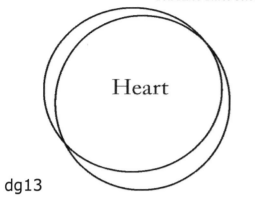

dg13

We have an adjective for persons exhibiting a large overlap of b/s and c/s, a large heart: mature. This is what we admire in healthy elders: maturity, the mutual acknowledging, acceptance and convergence of their mind and emotions.

This convergence can happen thru Grace. More often it happens, I find, thru being pro-active about resolving inner disturbances as they come up, not running away from them.

E&C: Committing to committing to yourself

We tend to walk thru life preferring ONLY our enteric or cerebral strategies. This is like walking thru life on one leg. Committing to committing to yourself means, sooner or later, committing to the rest of the human capacities you have, that got covered up in various ways. We can even get comfortable in how we are polarized, how we are walking around, hopping around on one leg.

.vVv.

3S 109: What each self does uniquely

Each of the three stations in the human psyche has responsibilities, functions and capacities designated to it. In adult-speak we'd say, each self has a job description.

HIGH SELF

The high self has no home in the physical body nor any physical home. Its station is above the physical head in a realm of higher frequency than the Earth plane. The high self's job is to maintain the station of the Spirit for you. It's domain is anything to do with the dim and dark areas above the conscious mind. We activate our h/s when we ask for spiritual assistance; or, have kept our spiritual gas tank full enuf that Grace can be extended according to our preferences. Prayer, gratitude and meditation are ways we put gas into our spiritual gas tank.

Experience your high self right now

Ever hear of luck? Find a good job or a valuable relationship you don't recall creating? Chances are good your High Self assisted in arranging things to work out to your benefit. Feel gratitude for your good fortune and you complete the circle and give back to those who have given to you. They give more to appreciative souls, you know.

Each soul is assigned a master consciousness always higher and more spiritually aware than the conscious mind of the person it is attached to. It embodies a capacity for overview and dispassionate objectivity. The high self is aware of the life plan chosen by the soul, the treasure chest of past abilities, acquired past tendencies; and, the karmic possibilities to be worked thru in this embodiment (Sanderson Beck, paraphrase).

Q: What does a guardian angel do?

A: An explanation of the Guardian Angel can distract us from the prime directive between the c/s and high self. To forge a closer personal connection with our h/s, and thru it towards our own soul, gratitude is the way up.

That said, here are the most tangible reference points for function per se. Our h/s communicates with, and keeps us connected with, our spiritual potentials, the dim and dark areas in frequencies higher than the conscious self. The h/s connects us with resources above the limited "I", with spiritual assistance, on an "as needed" basis: as we need it and as we ask for it. "Operators are standing by" as they say. The high self throws open the doors of Grace when the action is both possible and permitted.

"Spiritual assistance" are spiritual beings who wish to serve. That's how they earn their wings to fly higher.

These beings include other high selves, angels, Master Teachers, The Great White Brotherhood, etc.

How full is your spiritual gas tank?

How full your spiritual gas tank is, determines to some degree, the amount of grace that can be extended thru spiritual assistance to us. The c/s can't measure how full the spiritual gas tank is. It can only be measured from above, from the high self and higher.

Q: How do I put "gas" in my spiritual gas tank?

A: Thru good works and service; and, spiritual exercises. A spiritual exercise is anything you do with your eyes closed and your intention focused on connecting with your own Divinity. Spiritual exercises can be considered successful in how well you were able to reach above the yak-yak mind.

Q: Does everyone have a high self?

A: People who see this directly agree every person has one or more such helpmates in Spirit. These guides are with us whether we are aware or not. All guides around a single person, work closely together, and merge together from the c/s point of view. Our Friends in Spirit see all our strengths and weaknesses, disharmonies and joys, much clearer than we can see them ourselves because they are not limited by the physical as we are. "The high self is the utterly trustworthy parental spirit," says Alan Lewis (1984, p 20).

The Holy Group of High Selves

Your h/s talks with other high selves. Constantly. About what? Everything of significance between you and anyone else, issues of any size. The high selves are talking all the time. This is widely recognized in all of Huna, in Max Long and in John-Roger's material.

High selves are not bound by linear time the way the c/s is. The 3D level is the only place where time is strictly linear and flowing in only one direction. From above, the h/s can see ahead to the likely consequences of actions and decisions being made now. They can moderate consequences to the person according to the person's "Light Units" (John-Roger), your spiritual gas tank).

A lot of our good luck goes on invisibly. Just how many car accidents have you avoided in your life? Perhaps more than just those you were aware of.

Find the holy group of high selves in some movies

A certain genre of B movie was created in the 1970s expressing the holy group of high selves point of view dramatically and clearly. The premier example is unfortunately rather obscure. I have been unable to track it down. It is called something like Wreck on

Highway 69 (circa 1970s). I've watched it twice because it's so clear about the holy group of high selves point of view. The ABC TV series "Lost" inherits some of the legacy of this genre.

The high self point of view is visible in the structure of the script. The movie starts with a multi-car pile up on the highway, clearly a southern California freeway with a fictitious name. We see a twenty car pile up occur, all views from long shots. We see the crash from a distance with no personal details of the drivers and passengers. The crash is on a Sunday afternoon, I believe. Then the movie jumps back to the Friday before to the first things any of the people did that began the chain of events leading to the eventual pile-up. The movie follows the several cars and families, etc. and shows how they converge at the same time and place in the large wreck. The script does some connecting of the choices people make with the consequent wreck. The final wreck at the end turns into a long 20 minute chain of events which become excruciating to the audience due to foreknowledge of the wreck to come and the engagement we now feel with these participants. To some degree the good karma or lack of it is reflected in their behavior and injuries after the wreck.

This is how the high selves see 3D events and how they work together. If you are a high self, part of your job description is communicating with other h/ss about the value of interactions between your respective charge.

The h/s is not bound by linear time the way the c/s is. H/ss can see ahead to the likely consequences to actions and decisions being made now. They can moderate consequences to the person according to their spiritual gas tank.

What does the c/s DO?

As seen from Spirit, the conscious self is the Earthly reflection, the stand-in, here in 3D, for the immortal, eternal soul. The conscious self is not the same as the eternal and immortal soul. It is, however, the lens, or focus, or mirror for the soul here, for each individual.

So if you think you are God, you are both right and wrong. When in fifth grade, a young boy or girl goes outside with a magnifying glass and focuses sunlight to one-pointedness on the ground--that's how the c/s focuses the soul here. The Sun represents the soul; the child represents the conscious self; the human experience--that's the lens, bringing the soul to a point of focus.

The c/s reflects the soul's strengths and weaknesses. Things learned by the c/s accrue to the soul.

While 'soul is choice' and the c/s understands choice, at least after puberty, most of the c/s's time and energy is spent directing the mind, emotions and body. The conscious self is the one who

- picks which book to buy

- evaluates which friends to invite to lunch

- makes a household budget

- makes lists

- looks for lessons from the past, and

- makes concrete plans for the future.

At its best, when it can arrange things to remove distractions, the conscious self is the clear, calm place from which to make healthy decisions and healthy choices.

As we all know this more often than not looks like, 'make as many errors are you can and learn from every one.' "Growing up is the hardest job anybody ever has to do," as John Bradshaw says.

Ultimately, the conscious self's job depends on what you believe the purpose of life here is. That's your call, up to you.

The conscious self is the one who speaks, our voice. In the body, it's "home" is the throat, more generally from throat to the crown of the head. The c/s is the asker, the chooser, the decider and the completer in our life here (John-Roger).

An archetypal c/s experience is a bank teller transaction at the bank. A bank teller is being paid to stay conscious and not let anything escape outside the "light of day." When they count out those big greenback bills for you, they have to be conscious; you want them to be conscious. You want to be conscious also to check their work. Only the c/s can do that here in 3D.

Another c/s job is being the protector and advocate for the health of the basic self. How well or poorly the c/s protects and advocates for children, theirs or other's, reflects how that c/s gets along with its own b/s. The relationship is exactly analogous, by spiritual design.

Dysfunctional relationship between adults and children can be summarized as adults using children as the playthings of adults, children exploited to serve adult purposes and desires.

Dysfunctional relationship between the c/s and b/s can be summarized similarly. The c/s exploiting the b/s for c/s purposes. This can look like excessive focus and seeking for sensation, stimulation, distraction and escape.

We all require pleasurable experiences here. We call a healthy occasional escape a "vacation." Excessive vacationing is not the same as being the protector and advocate for the health of the b/s.

We have great opportunity here on Earth to practice

honoring, protecting and creating optimal health with our b/s.

The b/s is already in cooperation with the c/s. The c/s has to choose anew each embodiment to cooperate with the b/s for the highest good of all. You can choose to cooperate better now. That's the gift of choice.

The conscious self is the most separated self here 2

The basic selves and high selves are already always connected and communicating. They can and do talk to each other over great distances. The basic selves are often like kids in a sandbox, talking to each other according to who wants what or when one wants to give another a kiss or a hug. The high selves are more concerned with who is learning how much from whom; and, where the next opportunity for healthy choice is.

Our poor conscious self only feel fully alive in the crisp, clean, clear light of day. Heck, it even sleeps at night; the b/s and h/s do not sleep in the same way at all. The c/s only feels secure where things have at least comfortable definition and clarity, its comfort zone.

From the c/s perspective, the b/s and h/s live in dim, dark places; where things merge, boundaries are fuzzy, listening replaces vision, the favored tool of many c/ss. It requires courage on the part of the c/s to leave the 'light of day' and go into dim and dark areas of the psyche, curiosity and courage.

Q: If the conscious self is similar to the soul, why do we need a soul?

A: It's not the c/s who needs a soul; it's the soul who needs a conscious self. The conscious self likes to think it's IT, the big Boss. But without a person's soul, there is no need for a conscious self in that individual. The c/s is here because the soul is too amorphous, too undefined to imagine it can be limited to a physical body. The c/s can easily be conditioned to believe the body, mind and emotions are worth quality attention. The soul is not under this illusion.

Soul is choice

Loving is a choice and soul is choice. The conscious self is more about managing behavior and upgrading old habits in our habit body PACME.

Life experience on Earth is primarily experienced as training for the conscious self.

The b/s and h/s are already doing the best they can with what they know and what they have to work with. The c/s is the lever for change here. Thru its choices, the soul rounds out its excesses and deficiencies, the under- and overcharged aspects of the psyche it has allowed, promoted and created below soul.

The etheric body is the one who wants to do better next time (Rudolf Steiner). The c/s is the one directing habits and behavior over and over, until the desired result or alignment is produced. Neither the b/s nor the h/s has this responsibility. That's the lesson here in 3D: Make the very best decision you can right now. Make all the good choices you can every day. The conscious self is the center of governance of the three selves.

The c/s is being trained to initiate cooperation with the basic self and high self. Only the conscious middle self can initiate communication with other levels of consciousness. The b/s is the expert on the physical body, not the thinking mind. Yet good health on all levels requires quality management from the seat of governance, the c/s.

With kinesiology testing, the conscious self can learn to ask the b/s directly when the body goes out of balance. If we wait too long, physical PAIN reminds us we need to slow down and learn what is happening inside the body. The c/s is being trained to stay conscious and catch unresolved disturbances before they manifest as pain. This is where kinesiology testing has its highest use: catching energetic disturbances before they trickle down into the physical. See 3S 113 for more.

C/s is your accountable adult self

The responsible conscious self is the inner adult who

- is in touch with reality,

- can postpone present pleasure for longer term gain

- estimates the consequences of choices, and

- is accountable to others.

The conscious self is the accountable part, the keeper of your integrity, your integration. If there is a failure of integration or accountability, this is the one who feels the guilt.

"Adequate and sufficient domination" of the b/s

"Responsibility" is a continuum with two poles. At one end of the responsibility scale, the c/s abdicates all personal responsibility and delegates, delays, avoids as many decisions as possible. Some addicts given in totally to their addiction; and, some homeless persons who have given up any responsibility for taking care of themselves, express the dysfunctional pole of responsibility.

The other pole is also dysfunctional: control freaks who wish to make all your decisions for you as well as their own. These people interpret all assistance as interference.

You can see this scale operating with dog owners. Some dog lovers have conflicts over any house breaking of a puppy in their own home. It pains them to enforce any boundaries on behavior. At the other end are dog owners who drive themselves and their pets daily for six months to dog training academy to get perfect obedience. And then take dog obedience school all over again a second time.

A continuum of responsibility is visible in classroom school teacher styles, from unnecessarily strict to thoughtless and careless.

Q: What's healthy on this scale of responsibility?

A: Health is not any rigid position. Even moderation in all things--held rigidly--might not be healthy. Equally problematic is too few boundaries and structures. Moral relativism, do your own thing; anything goes, represent this position. The relevant myth is the lotus eaters who relaxed all day and never accomplished anything. This is just as much a problem for growth as over-rigidity.

Health is flexibility to respond from any point on the continuum of response-ability. The more ways we have to respond, the more options we have in responding to life.

Michaela Glockler, M.D. is a Waldorf school medical doctor and spokesperson for healthy impulses for children. She gives wonderful language to discuss the second problem. She calls it "insufficient domination of the will forces." "Will forces" is a 19th century term for what we call the basic self today.

In a lecture of hers I attended around 1990, she spoke of adequate and sufficient domination of the will forces by the conscious "I" as part of optimal health. This provides useful language for discussing addictions and compulsions.

Adequate and sufficient domination of b/s is a theme in many counseling modalities of the 1980s. After a decade of "do your own thing," cognitive and behavioral therapies of the 1980s made the point that dwelling on feeling good and prizing insight alone do not directly strengthen the cognitive faculties. Soul is choice. We are charged by life to improve in our capacity to choose, decide, and complete.

The basic self's "home" in our body is the solar plexus, our body's physical center of gravity. Its main interface is in the solar plexus, in the front of the body, below the sternum (breast bone). Strong emotions in our solar plexus ganglia, can trigger fight or fly reactions.

The basic self is in charge of the physical body in all material respects including and not limited to, reflexes and metabolic activity, down to digestion and assimilation. Which self handles cell division is unclear to me. Angelic beings perhaps? The b/s is the one who handles routine habits and behaviors so the c/s has room to think about what it's doing.

Below is a paraphrase of Sanderson Beck's version of some of John-Roger's ideas, on the b/s, from the "Self" section of Sanderson's web-doc, LIFE AS A WHOLE.

A little self-observation tells us we are not conscious of most of our bodily processes and instincts. They simply seem automatic. These processes are not mechanical, but richly alive. The basic self is often referred to as the 'lower self.' Its awareness of energetic pathways and boundaries in the body and aura is advanced and complex. ... The basic self comes out of a repository of basic selves and returns there after physical death (John-Roger). Basic selves are also in a process of evolution (John-Roger). It may be that some animals are evolving basic selves. Higher mammals, especially pets who live closely with humans, are approaching the state where they may be assigned as a basic self for a human body.

According to John-Roger, within twenty-four hours of conception, a basic self enters the fertilized egg within the womb of the mother. In any given embodiment here, the basic self is first responsible for developing the embryo and for maintaining bodily functions.

Genetic patterns of heredity, DNA, program in large part, the physical body the b/s is going to build. Once aware in the body, the b/s is further conditioned and trained through experience as well. In many respects the basic self is like a child. Like a young child, it is emotionally expressive. The b/s is easily trained by conditioning with rewards and punishments. It forms habits easily. These can only be changed by re-training, by upgrading old habits deliberately. The b/s has much wisdom–of certain kinds. The b/s is highly identified with feelings. Some b/s are extremely sensitive; others are less sensitive emotionally. To reach it, it must be appealed to at its map of its world.

From the c/s position, the basic self is sub- and unconscious. By practicing firm and kind parenting skills, the conscious self develops better and better communication with the b/s.

In the deeper unconscious mind, the lower self converges with the higher self. The two work together to bring forward and release disturbances--as the conscious self has tools and opportunity to resolve them.

"My basic self made me do it," is foolish escapism

We must also keep in mind...any separation is artificial. We are completely responsible for all levels of our consciousness. If I say," That was my basic self who did it, not me," it might be a joke. But if I mean the remark seriously, to get me off the hook of personal responsibility, if I blame my b/s for choices I have made, this is "passing the buck." ... This is irresponsible behavior (from

Sanderson Beck revised for clarity).

For better and worse the c/s has no one else to blame for its choices but itself. Knowing about inner child provides no scapegoat to blame for our poor choices.

When we screw up, sure, we don't like to be caught with our hand in the cookie jar. We don't want to feel responsible for our poor decisions. Unfortunately if the captain of the ship abdicates the helm and the ship goes off course, no matter how the captain explains or excuses himself, he's responsible.

Q: If the "basic self" is so basic, why haven't I heard of it before?

A: The basic self is widely and openly discussed in every eastern martial art practice known.

The basic self as center of gravity (hara, dan tien)

Every oriental martial art since antiquity, including tai chi and chi gung, the center of gravity in the body is discussed at length. Our physical center of gravity is discussed as the center of our physical vitality and physical healing energy as well. All this is of practical relevance in martial arts. This is the basic self.

Sometimes it's called the "hara." In chi gung this center is called the "dan tien." The dan tien has as many names and shades of meaning in Eastern martial arts and spiritual disciplines, similar to the diverse shades of meaning the words "sub-conscious" and "unconscious" have in western psychology. So the basic self is nothing new. What mattered to the East was the physical and energetic aspects; what matters in the West was making logical sense out of abstractions.

Our center of gravity is worth discussing. Half of our body's weight is above the vicinity of our belly button, half below. Our basic self is our center of gravity in more ways than one:

It is the center of gravity of our feelings.

It is the center of gravity of our subconscious.

It is the center of gravity of our behavior.

It is the center of gravity of our preferences.

It is the center of gravity of our habits.

A word on learning the 3S

Abraham Kawai'i, who studied directly with living Kahunas, puts the three selves into healthy perspective in an interview in Whole Life Times, June, 1988.

In my own personal training, we trained with the three bodies [selves] only in the first six months. So the three body, or three self concept, means to me we are still in kindergarten. In practice there is much more the sense all three selves are combined...The kindergarten instructor would naturally say "high self." But when you get up into the college bracket, they don't have to say "high self" anymore; [the oneness] is totally understood.

The b/s is the most active self here in 3D

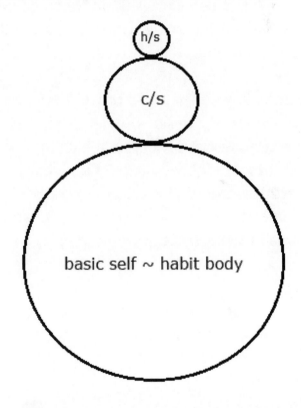

dg14

While in 3D, the conscious thinking self travels around like a gentleman in a cushy horse-drawn coach. The b/s is the one who performs all the walking, running, digesting, and so on. The head and neck, where the c/s is stationed, moves very little compared to our digestion and compared to our limbs and fingers (Rudolf Steiner, 1919).

Because the b/s is the most active self of the three here in 3D, some people believe this makes it the most significant self here. Not so. If the basic self was to run the show here, then we would never grow up. We would never grow out of old comfort zones once they are established. John-Roger has likened a person who allows their basic self to run their life to a five year old child allowed to drive an 18-wheeler truck. It might be able to do it, but not well. A crash is inevitable.

IF everyone allowed their b/s to run their life, then we have, the Planet of the Apes, where the basic selves rule. The popularity of this image lies in basic self interest in how things would be if the conscious selves were overthrown and basic selves were in charge. The Lord of the Flies (1954) in part comes to similar conclusions of what society would be like if children (b/ss) ran it.

For young persons before puberty, the basic self is the foreground of the human experience here on Earth. The conscious self is background.

The c/s is the most significant self here

This suggests the relative number and significance of 3D choices each makes. The c/s is the decider, the Chooser and the completer in all mundane affairs (John-Roger).

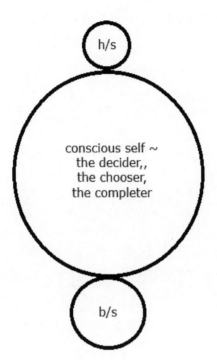

dg15

Prior to puberty, the basic self is foreground of the human experience here on Earth. In *The Inner Court* we'll talk more about how self-concept and self-esteem are converged in the basic self, in the gut brain, prior to puberty. At puberty, self-concept migrates up to the Inner Court in the head, establishes itself and becomes primary over self-esteem.

After puberty, the conscious self, and our self-concept, overlays our gut brain biography of self-esteem and becomes the foreground of our experience in 3D.

Once the conscious self becomes the foreground in

adulthood, the basic self and its biography of self-esteem becomes background.

The high self is the most active self in spirit

dg11

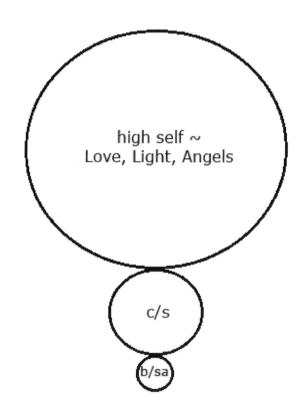

dg16

The mystery of magnets

Q: If the polarity between the conscious and basic self is so obvious, why don't I hear more about it?

A: You do. Ever hear of the north and south poles of a magnet?

Long known to magnet researchers, north and south poles both attract iron—and have unique and distinct properties as well:

North pole	South pole
sedates bacterial growth	stimulates bacterial growth
sedates sprouting seeds	stimulates sprouting seeds
aligns molecules in liquids	molecules more chaotic
alkaline forming	acid-forming
Blue and cool colors	Red and warm-hot colors

In human consciousness, the basic self is allied with all the qualities of South pole energy. The conscious self is allied with North pole qualities.

Many aspects of human personality can be listed in the two columns of North and South pole:

sympathy	antipathy
craving	aversion
fear	awe

worry	righteousness
activity	rest
possibilities	closure
youth	maturity
happiness, fun	joy, bliss
attachment	detachment
underachieving	overachieving
play (and lazy)	work (and control)
run habits automatically	changes and set new habits
inner child	conscious adult

So where's the high self? That's the part of you, looking at the magnet, viewing the polarity from outside and above, seeing the distinct qualities of each pole, understanding their gifts and limitations, seeing the two polarities as one whole--from a higher perspective. Your high self views your personality (basic self + conscious self) the way you view a magnet in your hand.

Q: What does the soul do?

Soul is the one with instant access to all qualities of beingness including honesty, loving, caring and sharing, wealth, riches and abundance, community, dancing and joy. These qualities are, in a sense, anti-matter; they are not conditioned matter. The soul is beingness; it touches all qualities at once; yet, the soul does express all qualities at once.

With the soul, we touch into quality; with the c/s we touch into the mind and some emotions; with the b/s we touch into feelings, needs and the Earth.

Detachment is the gold of 3D experience

The c/s is our ability to view 3D experience objectively. This is the good side of the c/s is the most separated self here, the positive side of looking in on life from the outside. The c/s is the one who makes useful distinctions. Making distinctions is a creative act (John-Roger). The c/s is the one who can distinguish, "I and my issue are not the same; I am not my issue, I am not my pain/hurt/disturbance." The practiced objectivity of the c/s can lead to the gold of detachment.
Detachment is the most valuable life lesson gained here in 3D, from Spirit's point of view, the most rare—and most useful--lesson learnable in 3D.

This is why in fairy tales, the unevolved, uncreative person is represented as the poor woodcutter. The uncreative person can only live by subtracting from life, subtracting from Nature's abundance. They have not yet evolved to some way of giving life, adding to life. They cannot yet bring forward any unconditional quality. The poor woodcutter is the one stuck--trapped--in conditioned reality, far away from royalty who all have more psychological freedom. The poor woodcutter perceives they must subtract from Life, to survive in 3D. They remain out of touch with unlimited unconditional energies of abundance until... thereby hangs a tale. In fairy tales the poor woodcutter begins a journey; events call forward his courage, independent thinking and other soul qualities. Thru this he outgrows his original station in life and is able to add to Life. This is represented as joining a royal family or line.

The 3S model is larger than most models of the human being. The human being is more magnificent than earlier philosophies and psychologies were able to articulate. Now we have the language to do so.

The conscious self as sense organ for the soul

20th century models of the psyche were notoriously conscious-self-centric, ego-centric, trying to explain everything in terms of the small "s" self; including, "How to get rich now!"

Our five most materialistic senses, smell, taste, touch, hearing and sight are sense organs for the conscious self. Very few of us confuse our sense of taste, for instance with "I am." Those who do, remind me of my Grandmother's words about her fifth husband, "He doesn't eat to live; he lives to eat." The rest of us make a stronger distinction between our sense organs and who we are.

Now take that up one octave. Ideally the conscious self, when purified, is no more nor less than a sense organ for the soul. At this level, we would not confuse the passing wants, desires, schemes and games of the small "s" self with the "I am" of the capital "S" self, the soul.

Most advanced idea in this book

The other day Maryann Castellanos mentioned a new idea. Thru my filters it sounded like this. From the c/s' point of view, when it is coupled with loving, in a spiritual marriage with the high and basic selves; then, there is really only the conscious self and a spiritualized inner child. At this point your Little Artist is also your Little Buddha, the Beloved, the Precious One who is also wise **when asked.**

As noted elsewhere, the b/s and h/s are more similar than different. It's only the c/s that is isolated.

For more on this see the "J" diagram in *Volume Two*; also, many recursive references in this book to the progression, the sequence of

- Conscious self thinks it's an island

- C/s uncovered there is a lower self and starts cooperating!

- C/s uncovered there is a higher self and starts cooperating!

- The c/s has easy access to b/s and to h/s thru the b/s.

...\vVv/...

3S 110: If we had NO helper selves

What if you had no other selves? What if it was just you, the ego, the conscious self?

Without a basic self, there could be no living flesh and blood body. If we were only a conscious self with no body, we would join dis-incarnate entities, those still wandering around the earth plan, after losing their physical bodies, on the Earth but no longer of embodied humanity, waiting for the Tunnel of Light to go to a more appropriate place in Spirit.

Q: What if you had a conscious self and a body, but no basic self?

A: If we had an Earthly physical body—and no support for it--we would be no more lively and mobile than a freshly deceased person. The basic self is literally what makes individual physical movement here in 3D possible and fun.

A person without a basic self would soon die. The basic self runs our metabolism and operates all bodily functions done sub- and unconsciously. It connects us with the body's needs to eat, exercise, avoid danger, procreate, etc. Readers may know persons with no hunger or no physical pain response are not long-lasting in the 3D world.

John-Roger tells a story that makes the basic self obvious. A woman in the frame of mind of "I don't need any help," told J-R, "I'm the master of my fate," and was proud of this. J-R suggested if that was so, that she use her independence to do something simple, like stop breathing for 60 seconds. In about ten seconds she gasped for air. J-R asked, "Who breathed you?" The woman did not know. J-R said the one you don't know is the one you are here.

The basic self keeps all our bodies coordinated

In the U.S. in 1850s a man was injured and, for a lark, agreed to the request of his doctors to insert a clear glass window in his stomach so doctors could watch from the outside, the process of digestion inside his stomach, a literal window on digestion. Usually we are content NOT to be fully aware of such routine metabolic activity. Such routine activity is delegated to another part of us. That's the basic self. It carries out a wide range of routine behaviors, most of which the c/s is dimly aware of at best:

breathing

digestion

chewing

walking

holding the baby while you talk on the phone.

The basic self grows, maintains and repairs the physical body. The b/s sustains all habits and routines set in motion by the conscious self. Everything we do 'automatically' and 'by reflex' is done by the b/s. Your b/s cares ceaselessly for you, 24 hours a day. The basic self excels at recording and playing back habits on multiple levels. It's capacity to do this is amazing and grows as we mature. Using this capacity to our healthiest advantage is a main lesson here.

The c/s delegates routine behavior to the b/s

You delegate routine behaviors to your b/s. This is healthy. At one time we learned consciously how to tie our shoe laces. The first dozen times a four year old is learning to tie shoelaces, you cannot talk with them about other things. Their whole attention is focused on learning the shoe lace thing. At some point the b/s grasps this routine sufficiently. Afterwards a child can tie their own shoelaces routinely and hold a conversation while doing so. Ability to do two or more activities at one time—it's a good deal! The basic self is "secretary" to the executive conscious self. Like a secretary the basic self handles many actions and functions the c/s would be unable to handle, thinking of one thing at a time, especially so if the phone is ringing, baby crying, pot boiling over and UPS guy at the door.

Rudolf Steiner put it this way. In standing, I raise my knee. The uneducated c/s thinks, "I am the sole cause of raising my knee." What happens physically to raise the knee? The fibers on the muscles on the top of the thigh have to bunch up. The contracting of the muscle fibers levers the thigh femur; the knee raises. The b/s is needed so the c/s does not have to think about all these physical causes and physical effects. The c/s is allowed to focus on the purpose of its actions; the b/s handles the mechanics.

More examples. Moving the body is even more paradoxical when the action is pushing down. To push down with your arm or leg, your muscle fibers have to bunch up on the far side away from the side you can see. If the conscious self had to be aware of bunching up to push down, movement would be complicated to the point where the cause and effect would be impossible to track.

Food digestion. If the c/s had to be aware of all the chemistry involved, how much of which enzymes to squirt on which foods at what time, clearly we would have little time to learn about how the Soul creates thru intention and attention.

Dividing cells, healing wounds, forming bones, moving blood cells and metabolism--think you have time to be in control of those? The c/s is allowed to focus on the intentionality of its actions. That's where 97% of our lessons are, learning what choices result in greater health for self, others, world... C/ss are learning to track intentions and their results--but we are spared from dealing consciously with a great deal of routine cause and effect. So the c/s is already always out of control of a great deal of our own activity here, the very routine and mundane repetitive stuff. The c/s is freed up to be creative! Like to watch T.V.! Wait a minute, some thing's wrong with that...

The above paraphrases Rudolf Steiner's 1919 discussion, bringing it into the context of the three selves.

Q: What if we had no conscious self?

Mental retardation

(autism, developmentally challenged)

Developmental delay, by whatever name–is diminished function of the conscious self faculty, that is not age-appropriate. I taught severely autistic children for four years and loved it. Prior to that, I taught in 80 special ed classrooms as a substitute , spent a summer at Camphill Copake and toured two other progressive Camphill residential facilities for developmentally delayed children and young adults. All our autistic kids have very reduced ability to choose, decide and complete. They especially lack motivation and ability to make choices. Severely autistic kids just sit there a lot--however a large fraction hear everything quite well, as normally as you and I do.

Autistic people characteristically avoid eye contact. Soul to soul contact is too strong for them. Lessened eye contact is a reliable indicator of a diminished conscious self function. They experience this as confrontational; the light is too bright for the selfhood they have. Even the Light of an average, normal conscious self is too strong a light for their weaker conscious self. They cannot stand up for themselves.

That's why they like television and computers. The "eye" looking back at them is less intense than you or I looking back at them. TV and computers are interactive without confronting them.

Lack of eye contact is a good measure until you come across those few individuals who are fully awake in a very compromised physical vehicle. Like Steven Hawkins, the astrophysicist. These souls make and hold contact with you not thru the eyes, whose muscles they may be unable to control. Rather, they make contact with you thru a combination of speech, writing, gestures and behavior. This can apply to cerebral palsy (CP) clients, as in the movie, My Left Foot (circa 1990). They may or may not be lovable, as the movie also suggests.

If we had no conscious self at all

Sleepwalkers. The literature suggests sleepwalking is explained by the basic self walking the body while the conscious capacity is out of the body during sleep. The basic self is still home in the body. It may decide to get up and be active. Abraham Lincoln was a famous sleepwalker. People meeting sleepwalkers report an entity who can sometimes speak but has very limited ability to hear what you are saying. Sleepwalkers who can talk often express anxieties and fears of a young child, indicating you are hearing the basic self speak.

Some children in specialized special ed classrooms, are severe cases, with multiple handicaps. Some of these children cannot make eye contact, cannot talk, is unable to grasp objects, and unable to hold their head up. When the c/s is unable to be the "captain of the ship" to any degree at all; then, all that is left –on this level here--is the basic self. The basic self can go on eating– if fed–and excreting. That's about it. Such cases of "vegetative state" reveal how thoroughly, faithfully and diligently the basic self carries out its basic responsibilities, as assigned, even if no one is home to do the "driving."

The high self in special needs persons

The high self does not go away in mental retardation. A few special needs persons even have angels for high selves. You know them when you meet them. All they want to do is love you and look into your eyes. We have

two at my special ed school now. They are delightful.
They make you forget all your troubles. All they want to
do is to love and be loved.

The topic of mental retardation as seen from a healthy
metaphysical perspective is only found, to my
knowledge, in Rudolf Steiner's volumes on the subject.
His ideas are employed practically in the worldwide
Camphill Movement.

If we had no high self

The h/s would be the easiest one to live without. So
you can ignore your high self. Jiminy Cricket may be
hollering in Pinocchio's ear, but Pinocchio can choose to
ignore him.

Ignore the h/s and it will still be connected, it will simply
be off doing more interesting things while you are
oblivious to it.

v\V/v

3S 111:

Angels save us from

boring art, music & poetry

The 3S is very useful to explain many phenomena difficult to explain any other way, such as...

My best ideas come to me in the shower

The New Yorker once ran a cartoon with a guy sitting at his desk, shirt and tie, pencil ready, waiting for a good idea. To assist the process, he had moved his whole desk into his shower. In the cartoon, the shower is on and running. He sits at his desk under the running shower, ready for ideas.

Q: Good ideas come from Spirit, they come from the high self directly to the conscious self, right?

A: Not exactly.

C/s contacts the h/s thru the b/s

Both John-Roger and the Kahunas say the h/s goes thru the b/s to get to the c/s. This is my experience too. In other words, new ideas come down from Spirit, into the b/s, in order to then come up into the conscious mind.

Why? Because the h/s and b/s are more similar than

different, both subconscious. The c/s is the most
isolated by design. It's access to spirit is therefore thru
the inner child, thru loving connection with the child
within.

This is why our best ideas come to us in the shower, or
on walks, or when physically active, in some way "self-
forgetting," where the c/s gets out of the way between
b/s and h/s. Rudolf Steiner mentions getting
Inspiration, Imagination and Intuition down into the b/s,
where it can come UP as visual, auditory, and
kinesthetic "images" available to the c/s--if you pay
attention.

In dance and some other movement arts, some of these
steps are skipped. Inspiration, Imagination and
Intuition can come thru directly and immediately.

The more clear the communication between c/s and b/s,
the more easily and often this happens. Conversely, the
more unresolved disturbances, disharmony, trauma and
mis-communication between c/s and b/s, the fewer
ideas from the h/s can get thru.

The bottleneck between our conscious self and Spirit
is--loving the child within, our basic self.

Our h/s is not having any problems connecting with a
healthy b/s. It's the willingness of the c/s to align itself
with what is coming thru the b/s from Spirit that is in
question. If the person believes they came up with the

idea themselves—Spirit does not care. Spirit already knows the c/s is the most isolated self and has lots of funny ideas about independence. Spirit wins service points for itself by getting thru and cares nothing for having its name attached.

Two good examples of how our best ideas come in from above are music and dialog written for plays on the stage. It's been said no music exists on Earth without the collaboration of angels with humans. Melody specifically is said to come from the angels, the best explanation I've heard for the origin of melody. Spirit is a higher energy potential than where we are when awake in the physical. For angels to inspire us with music or other creativity is, for them, like water pouring downhill. It's no effort. The problem is not, "Will we run out of music?" The problem from the angelic point of view is, "Is there anyone down there open to inspiration from above?" If you are open, they can use you.

Goethe's best poetry composed while pacing

Rudolf Steiner remarks about Goethe composing the best lyrics of "Faust," while pacing the floor and dictating them to a secretary. Contrast Goethe's poetry with the last boring textbook you had to read. Can you imagine how much more lively that textbook might read if the author had dictated it while walking, swimming, bicycling, etc.

The poems of Rumi, the best-selling poet in America for many years running, were dictated while he was whirling as the Dervish he was.

Exercise addicts are likely to know how joy often comes forward more frequently and more strongly during physical exercise.

Delta --> theta --> alpha --> beta

Biofeedback training in the 1980s offered more precise terms to discuss consciousness with. According to this model:

- All healthy adults function in the fastest beta range of brain wave frequency,

- Any relaxed state takes you to an alpha level,

- Children age one to seven characteristically operate in the theta range,

- Infants birth to age one are in delta where we also have deep sleep.

The idea of a range of consciousness is very useful. Personal experience and common sense suggest the biofeedback model of the psyche is too mechanical and diagrammatic to be of practical value to persons lacking electronics to monitor brain wave activity. The promise that biofeedback could benefit a large fraction of the population has yet to be fulfilled.

As part of a learning curve about the psyche, biofeedback was tremendous. Now we know the brain is never at just one frequency, one rate; our awareness changes moment to moment, travels up and down, within a familiar range--a comfort zone, if you like. Consequently now in biofeedback it's common to hear about "theta-dominant brainwave activity," denoting a living breathing range of frequency is natural and normal.

Experience suggests the b/s operates and can be contacted at the theta level; also, that practiced conscious selves can learn to hold conscious awareness at alpha, theta and even delta. In fact, many modern adults who have done much "working on them self" are in alpha or theta on a daily basis without even being aware of this.

Musical preferences suggest your c/s frequency

What kind of music you like highly suggests the frequency range your conscious self is comfortable with. More precisely: What kind of music you like reflects the comfort zone of your conscious self on the scale of delta to beta. This explains why people disagree over what music to listen to. Smooth jazz may be your cup of tea but put your neighbor to sleep. They may like polka music but you find it makes you "hyper." The caveat here is one person's favorite music may be primarily a c/s liking whereas the next person's favorite music may express their b/s preference and liking.

The radio dial, the range of stations, musical and talk, evidences how the population divides itself up in terms of the frequency range. People listen to the frequencies and rhythm they feel most comfortable in.

AM talk radio, especially all news all the time, is strongly beta. Smooth jazz is strongly theta and puts some people to sleep.

Note how people who like similar music tend to get along. Note how radio stations hire on air disc jockeys whose verbal patter paces the rhythms of the music being played.

Q: What if I like more than one kind of music?

A: Hurray! The wider and more diverse your musical comfort zone, the wider your comfort zone in brain wave frequencies; the wider your comfort zone in life. Celebrate diversity.

What about 1950's Charlie Parker style jazz?

Some readers will know 1950s Charlie Parker-style jazz as a music characterized by:

- improvisation,

- deliberate avoidance of any melodic line whatsoever, for long passages.

For some listeners this music is grating and chaotic. For others, it is freeing and exciting.

Some readers will recall the connection between free-form jazz and the beat poets of the 1950s. Free form verse without any structure of rhyme scheme was paralleled in the kind of improvizational jazz characterized above. Both celebrate the unedited impulse. Readers who lived thru the 1950s will recall that this was a needed counterpoint to the social and cultural repression of the 1950s, the era of the gray, corporate IBM man.

These expressions celebrated irrationality when mainstream culture in the West was repressing any trace of the sub- and unconscious

Today we can view "irrational" music and poetry as wonderful examples of expression limited entirely to the basic self, expression WITHOUT Inspiration, Intuition or Imagination, without spiritual collaboration of any kind. This is the b/s expressing itself without benefit of or interference from the c/s or higher beings of any kind.

In the L. A. Times, Nov. 16, 2005, Lawrence Ferlinghetti says, "My poetry had a very different aesthetic. . . . The Jack Kerouac school of disembodied poetics is, 'first thought, best thought,' where you write down the first thing that comes to mind, to get close to the essential being of yourself," . . . referring to the author of On the Road and The Dharma Bums. "My poems were not written that way. I think it can sometimes be 'first thought, worst thought,' unless you have an original genius mind. . . and everything that comes out is interesting.' With less original minds , the method [of 'first thought, best thought'] produces acres and acres of boring poetry. "

Angelic collaboration literally saves us from boring music and poetry. Only the angels and other spiritual beings can add melody, grace, harmony and beauty to music and poetry. Why? They collaborate with us to earn their wings. The angels progress spiritually by being of service--just like we do.

v\V/v

3S 112:

"The Plan" for human beings

Was there a Plan for how to go thru Earth life as human beings?

What the heck was it?

The high self looks down lovingly on us.

The conscious self looks out lovingly at the world.

The basic self looks up lovingly
at the conscious self and high self.

This Plan for happiness can also be expressed another
way:

The basic self trusts and looks up to the rational mind
for collaboration on concerns of mutual interest.

The rational mind in convinced of its limitations and
looks both down to its partner, the basic, self for second
opinions on Earthly things; and, looks up to the high self
for second opinions on matters involving other people
and the future.

The high self looks up to greater and higher Beings
when it has a question.

My guess is this plan was composed by the Angels and
reflects their idea of "normal."

Metaphysical literature highly suggests this is how
things are in the higher astral worlds and further above.

So what happens down here on Earth that leads to so
much UNhappiness?

The basic self colludes with the lowest frequencies of the rational mind and they work together on "taking care of number one" with no or little regard for the highest good of ALL concerned. The context of desire starts and ends with, "What's in it for me?"

The rational mind allows the materialistic wants, needs and preferences of the basic self to become its "god" and supports the basic self in getting what it wants, thinking, as permissive parents err, that once the screaming child gets what it wants, it will leave the harried parent alone. However once the demanding child learns how much power they have, the scenario repeats endlessly.

The high self in this unhappy scenario is never consulted at all and drafts further and further away from neglect. The result is more and more downward spirals on more and more levels.

CAN we turn this around? Yes.

What does it take?

It takes willingness to change, willingness to grow; in a phrase, willingness to mature.

The Plan intimates quite a bit about suffering Either we can suffer with the consequences of following the demanding child of the low self; or, we can suffer in a healthy way by bit-by-bit learning self-control, self-discipline and direct our three selves back into alignment with happiness--as the angels see it.

Emotional cause and effect

Another part The Plan, it's been said, is for humanity to learn cause and effect in the emotional and mental levels. You might think from science books, cause and effect applies exclusively and only to the material realm of material things. True, cause and effect in the physical level is easy to grasp: what goes up must come down. Why don't we teach this happens emotionally as well? Why don't we teach "pride" as flying "too high" in the mind and "false humility" as flying "too low" in our self-concept? I don't know.

Cause and effect in our psyche is easy to see once "new eyes" are developed to cognize patterns in this vein: keep feel sad emotionally for a long time, sooner or later eventually feel depressed physically.

Cause and effect exists on all levels PACME but it's EASIEST to learn HERE because here in 3D, causes always come before, and effects always come after. Part of The Plan is for us to learn this applies in the mind and emotions too, where it's easy to learn this.

To help us learn cause and effect, The Plan was to endow the human psyche with three stations of consciousness to better enable the immortal soul to experience itself—in microcosm—including cause and effect.

High self---Alert to anything happening above your conscious mind relevant to you and to determining the value of things. Also called the super-conscious, guardian angel, and many synonyms.

Middle self---Alert to anything happening consciously, wherever your attention and intention fall, that's where the c/s is. At its best, the c/s is your clarity, neutrality and love, the soul focused here, like a thru a lens.

Basic self---Alert in our 3D percepts primarily.

Another part of The Plan was how each soul would go thru their next embodiment. Sanderson Beck has a web-published text called, LIFE AS A WHOLE: Principles of Education Based on a Spiritual Philosophy of Love (san.beck.org/Life-Contents.html). Here's a paraphrased reworking of part of his entry on the high self.

During one 3D embodiment, millions of conscious choices are made which alter and define a person's life. A soul's life plan allows for branching expressions within the scope of one embodiment. The high self may arrange things subtly to encourage the person into certain avenues; and, arrange things to protect the person from events beyond the person's destiny this life. The higher self never inflicts, commands, directs, or chooses for an individual.

According to the best reports we can gather together, before we re-embody, each of us agrees to a plan of how things will likely to go this embodiment, an outline of what is likely to and not likely to happen in the present existence, a general outline of the life lessons your soul wishes to work on. This plan includes things like who we are likely to meet and what we are likely to accomplish. "Hmm, given my past experiences, I think I now most need to learn X, Y and Z." The h/s tracks opportunities for personal and spiritual growth within our reach. Soul is choice. We exercise soul by our free choices here.

This plan or map is not set in stone. It can be changed. The fastest way to change it is to work on yourself. The more strongly you can align yourself, on all levels, with the highest good for yourself and all concerned, the more stress can be taken out of your plan. If you learn the lessons set up as your "curriculum," life goes more smoothly here.

The h/s is happy when the c/s locates and takes hold of opportunities to grow. The h/s will follow the lead of the c/s, whether it chooses to grow or not. The h/s understands the soul will learn to make better choices one way or another, often thru experiencing the consequences of its choices.

A fairy tale about The Plan of our evolution:

Ann is a young infant, She looks up to adults around her

for nurturance, protection, support and guidance. Adults do for Ann what she cannot do for herself. Adults initiate Ann to gradually take on more tasks she can do for herself.

Young Ann copies worthy adult examples of how to do things here: walking, opening doors, riding a bike, etc. In time, Ann's conscious self comes into to its own. She begins initiating herself into new behaviors independently, like playing the guitar. Over time Ann becomes her own primary care giver.

Ann comes into adulthood. If she comes into adulthood with her loving intact and loving to share; then, it often makes sense to have, adopt or work with children.

Then the gifts of nurturing, supporting and guiding, that were taken IN by Ann when she was young, are now gifts she gives OUT, passes on, to another up and coming generation of children.

This is the Plan. We can all relate to it. The Devil is in the details you say? Well, yes, we all deal with the details in 3D.

As Ann's conscious self gradually comes into its own, over time, her inner child is not obliterated. It does not die or go away. That idea is simply cultural programming. Ignore it. The adult, every adult, differentiates into a conscious self and a basic self (inner child) and remains a working unit until physical death.

We hope the conscious self consults with the high self, but we can't guarantee it. Cooperation is a choice. If it does, all three selves work together in a person. If an adult does not consult with the high self–you still have your own inner child to take care of–in addition to any external physical children you care for. Sometimes we hear busy parents sigh relief as they take care of themselves (their own basic needs) for a change.

The Plan is an artistic creation and the sequential nature of left brain language is unlikely to ever do it justice. That's why the Plan is so seldom seen written down – but the Plan is commonly visible in poetry and novels, especially inter-generational novels.

.:i:. .:i:. .:i:.

3S 113: Source code

for kinesiology testing

Muscle testing is not primarily about muscles!

The basic self is the one in charge of our muscles, not the thinking mind. Rudolf Steiner pointed this out in 1919. He suggests an experiment: hold up your finger and tell it with your mind to move; only use your mind, nothing else. Does it move? No. Until language for the basic self became available, scientists described this phenomena, that you can only move your finger by moving it, as "will" and "willpower."

Kinesiology testing is simply accessing the response of the basic self thru, for instance, muscle response.

Q: How is it possible for the basic self to test things in closed containers and long distance?

A: Because the basic self is a subset of the larger etheric bodies of the Earth, solar system, etc, it is relatively easy for it to tap into information from these larger versions of itself.

Kinesiology testing works well in practice;

it simply doesn't work well in theory.

That's one problem I hope the present book clears up. The 3S is source code here; it supports KT by providing the theoretical underpinning, the WHO and the HOW, to make K-testing understandable to college freshmen and any wishing to learn it in the context of 'God is my Partner.'

Earlier theories, from the 1930s thru 1990s, attempting to explain how dowsing, EFT and K-testing work in theory—without the 3S--inevitably became tangled up over muscles, phenomena, and general confusion, attempting to describe phenomena occurring between TWO nervous systems as occurring in only one nervous system.

This is why VAKOG is essential to understand as part of how K-testing works.

Arm-pull-down is the hardest way to test

Arm-pull-down, the best known form of muscle testing, is by far, the most difficult testing to do because it involves the most variables by far. Arm-pull-down taught as scientific" is responsible for more skepticism and cynicism about KT than any other factor.

Should arm-pull-down be banned?

No, it's quite useful if it's done in the form John-Roger brought forward, which I call Client-controlled Testing (CCT) where the testee is the sole and only person deciding HOW the test is done and WHAT test results mean. The arm-presser says nothing and does nothing to determine or evaluate the outcome or result of any test. This is honoring how each person tests uniquely and how self-testing is primarily valid in the domain of one person.

Kinesiology testing as seen thru the 3S

Muscles do not respond. The basic self responds using muscles—or something else—to respond with.

The essential presupposition of KT is this: the immune system is plenty smart enuf to know if a stimulus is "true for me now" (beneficial) or "not true for me now" (not beneficial).

Our immune system, your immune system, makes exactly this determination many thousands of times each day in our small intestine. To ask it this question on a bottle of vitamins is not asking it to do anything it has not already done millions of times. Mostly the issues is, does it trust you, the conscious self, enuf to voice and share its opinion with you?

The activity of experienced dowsers, kinesiology and self-muscle-testers can be expressed as a sequence of interactions between b/s and c/s:

1. A clear communication language structure of some kind (this response means "yes;" this response means "no," etc) already exists. The b/s trusts the c/s sufficiently to "voice" its responses to the c/s.

2 The self-tester surrenders control of the cerebral head brain nervous system, and its striated muscles, to the b/s, the enteric gut brain nervous system, and its smooth muscles.

3. The c/s composes and asks the b/s a clear question on a tangible topic; for example, "Is more fish liver oil beneficial or this body, at this time?" The conscious, waking, thinking mind relaxes all pre-conceptions as it is asking a question of another being, just like you would ask a reference librarian to learn something new.

4. If the basic self feels both safe and comfortable responding, it employs the pre-determined language signals.

5. The conscious self-tester evaluates responses in terms of which way more energy is flowing, which direction is more aligned with the highest good of the body.

The initial condition of safety is worth expanding on. All K-testing goes more smoothly if the operator takes time at the beginning of each session to set an intention of safety, precaution and protection. Asking for the Light of the Highest God and Greatest Loving, to fill, surround, protect and guide the tester and all involved is one form of psychic protection. The intention to align with the highest good for all concerned is the crucial element, not the words, not the ritual.

This can be done in any jargon comfortable to the tester. Making an explicit request for assistance facilitates the basic self to feel both safe and comfortable so it can share its "point of view" with the c/s.

Muscles are only a response mechanism of the basic self in testing, nothing more. More subtle, more inward responses can also be used by sensitive testers. See 20 more different ways the basic self can use muscles and the body to signal its responses, including burping, in , "Deviceless Dowsing" by Dan Wilson, posted many places online.

Training issues in K-testing

I find people can be trained to do self-testing in from five minutes to one hour. The ideal student of KT has:

- high willingness to learn

- is in touch with their own body percepts

- trusts their own body percepts.

K-testing has been around completely open and publicly since the early 1970s with Touch for Health. It's about the most useful thing you can learn given its 12 or more beneficial side effects, all related to supporting you thinking for your self. HealingToolbox has this article somewhere.

Why are so few people practicing KT?

One bottleneck is training protocols. The majority of trainers are iNtuitive Thinkers, very interested in the *system* of testing. However—the majority of students are iNtuitive FEELERS, mostly women, interested in connection with their own habit body and with other people. How "scientific" KT is or isn't doesn't interest them much. They simply want to *feel energy moving*. So training should focus on the direct experience of energy moving. This is what makes it "real" for folks.

The following remarks apply more or less equally well to the question, "Dowsing has been around and openly public since the 1930s. Why don't more people learn to dowse?"

iNtuitive Feelers also need a couple things few training protocols in KT offer.

For one, they need a lower "ramp" of competency. They need "competency" redefined as "able to connect with your own immune system." Not: able to test vitamins, food, water, clients; or even more problematic: ability to test the universe, books, movies, historical figures.

Second, based on my experience training folks, most people need to start with feeling safe. Period. Do I feel safe to test now? Ultimately feeling safe is not just the emotional permission and affect of the trainer; rather, it's instruction on how to work with Light, Love and

Angels as your Partner, so the Light does the heavy lifting not you, the small "s" self, the ego.

In testing, you are opening up your etheric centers. How will you protect yourself? If you "always use love all ways" (John-Roger) you will be automatically protected because Spirit protects its own.

Third. people need permission and practice to learn to trust their own sensory percepts. Bernard Gunther, who I had the pleasure to meet and talk with, wrote the seminal book on sensory awareness, *What to Do Until the Messiah Comes* (1971). It too is in the mood of playfulness. Rudolf Steiner's topic of the twelve senses helps people at this stage also, helping them reframe in a larger—frame—their perceptual capacities.

Awakening to our perceptual sensitivities, our most open channels of sensory perception, is at the heart of *Self-healing 101! Best Practices in Healing System; How to Talk with Your Immune System* (2009) the only book I know so far that fills this gap in the training protocol of K-testing.

If you know of other books that bridge this gap well AND discuss adequate and sufficient protection routines for students, please do let me know immediately.

Fortunately this lower ramp, a gentler, more sustainable way to introduce people who wish to learn to test to self-testing is now written down *in Self-Healing 101!*

Best Practices in Healing System; How to Talk with Your Immune System at Amazon and Kindle.

Feeling safe to match feelings to thots > curiosity and self-permission > self-sensitivity > self-trust > Intuition. See *Self-Healing 101!* For a more complete version.

"I don't trust my own testing."

After basic training, the biggest bottleneck in training is trained persons giving up on testing because they do not trust their own testing results.

Difficulties in testing often stem from a lack of creating, at the start, a clear intention of safety, love and support for all involved.

Troubleshooting these issues is one of the more interesting tasks trainers are asked about. It leads into the very fruitful area of "you have two minds—and this is a good thing!" Learning to trust your own testing more involves discerning when you yourself are of two minds—or not, how aligned are your thinking mind and feeling mind on the target you have in mind? This raises a large number of fruitful inner cooperation issues.

.:i:. .:i:. .:i:.

3S 114: Any dangers

in learning this material?

Yes, there are. Professional ethics must be applied everywhere in using the 3S. A constant danger is using information to control and manipulate others for the practitioner's agenda. Showing off is the mildest form of this. I've spent years working out my Mr. Know It All issues. If you use this book to feed your Know It All--I'll be sad.

Ethics exist to tell us where healthy boundaries for behavior are. Life is like a rubber band. If you stretch it beyond the boundaries of the highest good, life snaps back at you.

The next big danger of exploring dim and dark material is you are groping in the dark. You never know--unless you ask the client's unconscious--if you are bumping against unresolved trauma that if released too quickly, can precipitate the client into a healing crisis. If you are facilitating, and a healing crisis occurs, you will be held responsible for any damage done to the client. You may even be legally liable. I'll spare you stories I've heard.

The Law of Gentleness

My solution to this is to always ask the client's first three etheric centers if they can handle a proposed intervention or change.

Forcefully surfacing unresolved trauma became a topic when errors were made in the infancy of hypnotism, in the 1800s thru the 1950s. In the 1970s, some Rebirthing practitioners thought cathartic release is always good. This is nonsense. "Cathartic release is always good," is a bias. The only thing that is always good is the highest good for the client, practitioner and all involved.

In cathartic-oriented Rebirthing, the leader asks a participant to lie down, to breathe rapidly for the purpose of hyper-ventilating; and, to relive their earliest memories and/or birth experiences.

Okay...there is a lot to be learned from birth and trauma generally. Birth is the greatest learning experience. The topic at hand, tho, is the dangers.

If you hyperventilate lying down, an oxygen surplus develops; regardless, of what your mind is focusing on. An oxygen surplus always tells your cells, "time to dump the trash!" The cells start dumping old toxins and debris, whatever they can release and let go of. In this dumping, your cells can also dump old toxic memories, old cell-level memories. Some of these memories are old traumas; some can be big traumas.

If you have such traumas held in your cells, hyper-ventilating will FORCE these memories up and out. Pushing and dragging them out this way tends to force them out.

This is the principle Rebirthing and many other breath work modalities operate on. I'm NOT recommending this approach as a deliberate strategy because Force is not respectful to the conscious self and its capacity for choice. If it happens spontaneously, that's usually safe.

Q: Why could surfacing memories be unsafe?

A: It's possible the shock of previously hidden memories rushing back into awareness or even into the inner child, will shock the system and re-injure cells. The shock of extreme emotions remembered without tools to process them forces high voltage energy thru the cells without consideration to what they can handle. This can seriously damage physical tissues. In at least one recorded instance, the shock was strong enuf, to give a young person a stroke; yes, even a young person. That's how strong these energies can be.

I don't want to be responsible for forcing high voltage memories thru the cells and possibly causing them harm; do you? So any therapeutic modality that praises cathartic release unreservedly makes a basic error, a major safety error: believing that reliving all trauma is always good for you. Reliving trauma is only beneficial and healthy if and only when the client can learn from it. This is not always the case at all.

Curiosity alone is not a good reason to relive and release trauma.

The human psyche is designed and constructed by angels. They built in various protections and safe-guards. One of these is provision for when, in childhood, we undergo serious trauma and have too few tools and no safe place to process the emotions and integrate the learning. The angels hold this trauma for us in "suspended animation" in the unconscious, store it in a place in the physical body, and there it rests until the conscious self becomes curious: "Doctor, I have this pain in my back..." Maturity in the face of unresolved issues means having both the willingness to heal; and, the tools to surface, resolve, and clean up powerful currents of feeling the client was unable to resolve when younger.

So monkeying around in the 3S and in the inner child presents danger of stumbling onto unresolved issues and traumas you had forgotten about and did not know you had. If these are surfaced prematurely, you force the inner child to relive the trauma, possibly re-injuring yourself, and may force the inner child to repress the material again, making it even more difficult to get out.

How the angels clear trauma

What the angels suggest thru several channeled sources is, when counselors and healers encounter hidden strong feelings or traumas in a client, that the practitioner always ASK if the client's body needs to re-experience this, for a healing to take place. Sometimes the educational component is necessary to heal-- sometimes not. The trauma may have a lesson for the person. Sometimes the person needs to re-experience the old trauma *only somewhat* in order to learn from it. Then they can release the negative portions. If trauma releases successfully without the client knowing what's going on, that's grace.

How do you know which traumas have an educational component and which can be released thru Grace? You don't. YOU don't. The angels DO know. That's why ASKING is useful.

If asked, sometimes the angels will reply, yes, the issue can be cleared by them without the body re-experiencing the trauma. Always go with Grace if you can get it. If the person does not need to re-experience a trauma, then why go there? Take the healing and be grateful!

.vVv.

3S 115:

Aligning with your own high self

First you have to align with your own basic self, the child within. Do that, feel the loving, and the high comes in automatically.

If "Not my will but Thine be done" is your goal, then first you have to inner-cooperate with your basic self on matters of diet, health and sleep.

Not everyone is interested in embarking on a path of self-mastery. There's no hurry to do so. Who does it and when they do it is very individual.

Slowing down and asking for a second opinion from our lower helper self really is a step forward on a path of self-mastery.

I started small. In the early 1980s I started by asking which of two movies might be more enjoyable for me to go see. This was a choice-decision I had always made consciously before. When I found out how well asking worked, and confirmed poor choices turned out poorly, I now rarely pay for a movie without asking its value for me from my Partner.

Readers may know people who talk like this, "I don't make any decision without asking my pendulum first." As long as we don't make this into something rigid, unbending and mechanical that may be the side to err on until you have more confidence in your own decision making.

What really "turned me on" to the reality of Spiritual Assistance, a connection I could submit questions to for a second opinion, was not the asking, not the pendulum practice. I had been asking for years that way. Rather what turned me on was to express gratitude to the Beings who were so clearly assisting me. In expressing my gratefulness, I could feel the response beyond just getting a "yes" or a "no."

There might be some other behaviors a conscious self might try to align them self with the ideal of a Spiritual Warrior. What comes to mind is:

- Practices making healthy decisions, for themselves and for everyone involved,

- Self-evaluates their own decision making,

- Invites and encourages feedback from others on their behavior,

- Exercises the value, "Check Spirit constantly" (J-R) as a guide for decisions. Why? Because people here in 3D can only see each other from "I" level. Spirit does not have this limitation. The Beloved's intention is always service for the highest good, a viewpoint always worth consulting.

- Makes efforts to bring the following into all interactions, to the best of their ability:

acceptance > understanding > compassion >

forgiveness > negotiation > resolution > love

I find the above is much easier to bring into my interactions when I practice using what I'm learning in Nonviolent Communication (CNVC.org).

- Is mindful of alignment as converging the thinking mind and feeling mind into movement towards a common goal, keeping a sense of moving towards what you want more of.

- Likes the idea, 'soul is alignment.' Beyond "you are what you eat," "you are what you drive," and "clothes make the man," is you are what you align yourself with.

Intimacy as into-me-see

Consequently
the only way to have mature intimacy
with a partner,
male or female,
is to discover the love
you have inside yourself with the Beloved,
to feel it,
and allow another person in
to share it with you.

Then you hope you get lucky
and find a partner
who does the same with you.
This is true for both men and women.

So if you WANT TO GO FASTER IN SELF-HEALING, you slow down and give more time and attention to these activities above, another paradox of growth.

If you get stuck give me a call.

Tools That Heal Press

Best Practices in Energy Healing System
Resources by and for kinesiology testers and self-healers in all therapeutic modalities
HealingToolbox.org ~ HealingCoach.org ~ 310-280-1176 between 8 AM and 9 PM PST

All books written in an interactive, FUN style by a practicing Medical Intuitive with training from MSIA, USM and Waldorf teacher training from Rudolf Steiner College.

All books available in PAPER or EBOOK at Amazon, Kindle, Smashwords, etc.

Your Habit Body, An Owner's Manual

Our Habit Body is our best and closest friend. It remembers every routine thing we do daily--so we don't have to relearn all our habits all over again each day. Habits are reactivity set on automatic, behavior conditioned to repeat.

If this is so, how come the one thing human beings do better than anything else is to make the same mistake over and over and over again?

Based on results, we don't know as much about our habit body as people think. We need new Tools That Heal to get at the 90% of our habit body that is sub- and unconscious.

We have habits on five personality levels: physical,

imaginal, emotional, mental and unconscious. How are they organized? How do we keep all our habits organized so when we wake up in the morning, we don't have to relearn everything? Personal-spiritual growth is upgrading our habits on any of these levels. Sound like a lot to manage? This makes your job easier, the missing manual for anyone who owns a Habit Body.

We used to say, "He who doesn't know his history is doomed to repeat it." We can say more precisely, "Whoever neglects their habit body will have the same behaviors and results tomorrow, as they did yesterday." Find answers here:

• Why we were more lovable when we were young

• Every day we are "training a new puppy"

• Why 90% of habits are invisible in 3D

• A dozen common terms for the "habit body."

Garrison Keillor says, "Culture is what you know is so by age 12." ALL culture can be seen as just a bunch of habits, including your own. Once you can see it, you can redirect it. 78 pages.

Self-Healing 101! *Best Practices in Healing System; How to Talk with Your Immune System*

Eight original simple exercises for lay persons, healers and coaches about FEELING SAFE TO TRY NEW THINGS, Permission to feel, Permission to think, Permission to match feelings and thoughts; and, PERMISSION to ask Love, Light and Angels to be your Partners in all your testing. From this foundation, teaching any method-technique, including kinesiology testing is a cinch. Self-sensitivity, self-trust and feeling safe lay the foundation for Intuition and willingness to heal. For lay persons, coaches and practitioners of energy healing and energy medicine.

The common denominators of Touch for Health, NLP, Theta Healing, Psych-K, and especially PTS Master program, are self-sensitivity, self-trust and Love, Light and Angels. Start with those and any technique-method, including kinesiology testing becomes easier.

Success at Intuitive development training needs to be measured by whether students trust their own test results three weeks after a class. Do they? If not, permissions and safety were not addressed adequately. 40,000 words 179 p. in 6x9 format.

Meridian Metaphors,

Psychology of the Meridians and Major Organs

Ever wonder what the connection between meridians, organs and emotions is? Ever think TCM had a start on good ideas but much was missing? Now anyone can work either forwards or backwards, between disturbed organs and meridians on one hand; and, disturbed mental-emotional states on the other hand. All descriptions begin with healthy function. Disturbances are further categorized by under- and overcharge conditions. Includes the myths and metaphors of under-overcharged organs-meridians condensed from Psychological Kinesiology plus much new material from other clinical practitioners. 22,000 words 80 page manual, 8 x10"

"Willingness to heal

is the pre-requisite for all healing"

This quote from Bertrand Babinet begins exploration and expansion of some of Bertrand Babinet's wonderful legacy of theory and method.

If you can do kinesiology testing by any method, you can measure your own willingness to heal. Self-testers can measure their own willingness to heal, in your inner child.

This tells you if your silent partner is ready to heal what you wish to heal. You can use this to explore where you are most ready to grow.

Have clients? The effectiveness of any energetic session can be estimated AHEAD OF TIME, with surprising accuracy--before you begin working! Practitioners in any and all modalities, are encouraged measure willingness to heal FIRST!

Save your self from wasting effort when clients are of two minds on their issue and do not know this. The higher the number on a scale of 1-10, the more momentum your client has to heal on that issue.

Willingness to heal is the key to aligning and integrating the three selves. Willingness is where the whole topic of the 3S leads.

NOTE ~ This booklet assumes readers can already either self-test using kinesiology testing—K-testing, dowsing, or some other form; or, can follow instructions to use any partner to do two-person testing, termed

Client

Controlled Testing. Problems with your own testing? Don't trust your own results? See the training protocol breakthroughs in Self-Healing 101! Awakening the Inner Healer.

You Have Three Selves; *Simplest, clearest model of the Whole Person Volume ONE, Orientation*

Compose your own vision of self-healing with the first comprehensive general textbook on the Three Selves. The basic self is functionally equal to the inner child, Little Artist, immune system and 12 other 20th century terms. The conscious self is your rational mind, which can be either feeling or thinking! Your high self is your guardian angel, your own higher Guidance. Aligning all three of these on the same goal so they can work as a team, describes much of what we do in 3D embodiment. Written with diagrams and much humor. 223 p. 6x9"

You Have Three Selves; *Simplest, clearest model of the Whole Person; Volume TWO, Finding the 3S in Your Life*

If the Three Selves are universal and pervasive in psychology, they ought to be visible all around us. Yikes, it's true! Find the 3S in your body, in pop culture, in the fun of Transactional Analysis, etc. 93 p. 6x9"

The Inner Court: *Close-up of the Habit Body*

The four archetypal characters, Guinevere, Lancelot,

Merlin & King Arthur (GLMA) are all alive and well-- inside each of us. They function as our Inner Court influencing our habits, behaviors, and comfort zones. All their expressions, both functional and dysfunctional, described in detail in Arthurian legend, are a close-up of possible behaviors and expressions in the basic self.

This is a map of inner child, four times as precise as Bradshaw's unitary concept of the "inner child." All insights are easily transferred to working with clients.

GLMA do not determine personality. Yet, our likes & dislikes, strengths & weaknesses, functional & dysfunctional expressions are all "written" in our Inner Court—until we upgrade the habitual patterns each follow.

We have TWO Inner Courts, one in our gut brain, a second on in the four quadrants in the brain. These make the previously mysterious topics of self-esteem and self-concept understandable.

The Inner Court also makes clear the strengths and weaknesses of:

- MBTI, how personality is formed thru preferences,

- Aristotle-Rudolf Steiner's four Temperaments; and, all other temperament and personality typology systems. The work of Katherine Benziger is clarified and made more artistic.

- How personality transforms thru personal & spiritual growth.

- The promise of earlier research on Right and left brain blossoms fully in the Inner Court.

Dysfunctional expressions of the Inner Court are clearly listed, providing a map to locate where everyday disturbances originate and track back to. If you can feel it—and locate it--you can heal it! All aspects of the Inner Court lends itself highly to muscle testing experiments.

The Inner Court model is appropriate to grad students and ANYONE interested in counseling, coaching, training, sales and personal growth. 116 p. 6x9"

The NEW Energy Anatomy:

Nine new views of human energy

that don't require clairvoyance

The Three Selves is simply the clearest, easiest map-model for the whole person. Here's the greater detail you would expect in an anatomy that goes with the 3S.

An easier, simpler, faster way to learn about human energy system compared to the chakra system. The NEW Energy Anatomy is a better entry point for students to developing sensitivity. Each view is testable with kinesiology of any and all kinds. You be the judge!

Physical anatomy is used by every effective energetic practitioner and self-healer. When your target is invisible, as often true--the best map is invaluable!

Maps of chakras, auras, acupuncture points, and reflex points are common—and commonly confusing to students because they cannot be perceived directly without clairvoyance. If you ARE clairvoyant, these aspects are easier to perceive and lead into the even deeper symbology of the chakra system.

These nine simpler views replace the chakra system as a starting place for most students of human energy. Each one is testable with kinesiology of any method. See for yourself!

NEW Energy Anatomy replaces some of the older views of human energy with views much simpler to visualize

Particularly useful for energy school students and sensitive persons using testing to sort out their abundant perceptions. More generally useful for efforts to become more Coherent, Integrated and Aligned (the *new CIA*). Coupled with Touch for Health, EFT, Energy Medicine or PTS Masters and Doctorate programs, these views facilitate making your aura brighter.

Human energy is organized:

1) Right and left in the body, yin & yang in the body.

2) Top and bottom, enteric and cerebral nervous systems.

3) Front and back, CV-GV, Clark Kent and Superman.

4) As frequency, best viewed as four kinds of laughter!

5) Our gut brain has two frequencies, divided top and bottom, feeling above (hey, hey hey!) and willingness below (ho, ho, ho!).

6) Our inner child has four distinct quadrants, an Inner Court.

7) We have a second Inner Court in our head.

8) The back of our head is willingness to heal our past.

9) Hip stability is a Ring of Loving you can strengthen.

Other material includes the Law of Gentleness for

healers, coaches & counselors. 25,000 words.

The Five Puberties, *a Three Selves Journal on Children*

Growing new eyes to see children afresh is the goal of this booklet. It builds on the foundation of the other volumes—or--can be read alone. Children are viewed thru lenses not often used: body posture, stories the body tells, animals, plants, the succession of puberties-- at least four puberties--each of us undergoes on our journey towards independent thinking.

Finally, we glance at what progress has been made towards a functional typology of children's temperaments in Anthroposophy, MBTI and Katherine Benziger, providing some directions for fruitful further study. The perplexing problem of how children's typology differs from adult typology, is brought close to resolution.

Radical Cellular Wellness—Especially for Women!

Cell psychology for everyone;

A coherent theory of illness and wellness

Finally a Theory of Illness and a Theory of How We Heal for everyone—especially for women: your cells are born healthy; and left on their own, cells remain healthy and reproduce perfectly. It is only environmental and human pollution that interferes with cell health and reproduction.

The various forms of internal pollution we allow,

promote and create are discussed with an eye to solutions!

How We Heal; and, Why do we get sick?

Including 35 better, more precise questions on wellness and healing, answered by a Medical Intuitive

Why every illness is a healing metaphor A theory of Cellular Awakening, short version.

Your personal beliefs & myths about healing.

#1: If we understand our problems, they will be healed.

#2: If you don't know and don't understand, then you can't heal.

#3: Personal-spiritual change takes a long time and is always a slow process. After all, you've had the problem for a long time.

#4: If you've had a negative belief for a long time, it will take a long time to change.

#5: If you change quickly, it must be superficial and not long lasting.

#6: I can't change; "This is the way I am; I'll always be this way."

#7: If you are middle-aged or older, it is too late to change.

#8: Changing old behaviors and thought patterns is often difficult and painful, "No pain, no gain."

Why is pain allowed? Why do I put up with so much pain in my body?

Can you help me see disease from Spirit's point of view?

18 more questions--answered!

You have FIVE bodies; *Spiritual Geography 101*

A fundamental distinction John-Roger and others make early and often is the useful tool of Spiritual Geography, discerning we have not one body here on Earth, but FIVE. Take away or compromise with any one of these bodies and we become less than fully human, less than fully capable of giving and receiving love. Topics include:

What makes us human is primarily invisible

Experience your five bodies RIGHT NOW

Two simple spiritual geographies

The map of Creation in your own hand

PACME ~ CIEMU: low frequency to high frequency

Tiger's Fang & When Are You Coming Home?

CIEMU can also be concentric circles

We have habits and comfort zones on each level CIEMU

Can I measure the soul here in 3D?

Can I see the soul here in the 3D world?

How does Spirit view my illness?

Where does physical disease come from?

Where are the primary causative factors of illness?

Only two kinds of problems

Why is the outer world more compelling than the inner?

Redeeming the imagination

The Meaning of Illness is Now an Open Book;

Cross-referencing Illness and Issues

Did you know FIVE books exist by different authors, cross-referencing illnesses and mental-emotional issues? Find summaries and reviews here. Illness as a healing metaphor. Willingness to heal is the pre-requisite to heal ~ What I see as a practicing Medical Intuitive ~ Connecting the dots between your illness and your issues. Ten illness patterns looked at from the Three Selves point of view. Additional disease patterns known by readers are welcomed for the second edition. 13,000 words 50 pages in 8.5x11 format.

Holistic Chamber Start-up Kit (2009 edition)

Everything you need to start your own local Holistic Chamber of Commerce .A fundraiser for local HCCs everywhere!

Each copy purchased benefits the local Chamber you buy it from. Bruce Dickson, Founder, Co-Chair ToolsThatHeal.com ~ HealingCoach.org

Camille Leon, Co-Chair ~ WAVEgeneration.com Westside Holistic Chamber of Commerce & HolisticChambersUSA.com

8,000 words to inspire you to start a local chamber, where the network is, tips and hard-won experience to save you time on the front end. Concludes with some ideas you can implement once you get going.

Other products

Slow-Motion Forgiveness ™ Practice CD

The Five Puberties, a 3S journal on Children, 40 p. 6x9"

Your Illness Is Now an Open Book, Free 31 page PDF by request.

Muscle Testing Practice Group DVD. One hour.

Rudolf Steiner's Fifth Gospel in Story Form

(140 pages). PDF available for free by email request.

1:1 phone sessions available. Group classes available. Training to do what I do is available.

Other CLASSICS of self-healing
& Medical Intuition

Our Many Selves, Elizabeth O'Connor

Touch for Health, 2nd Ed, Mathew Thie

Your Body Speaks Your Mind, 2nd ed. Deb Shapiro

Core Transformation, Connierae Andreas

Forgiveness, Key to the Kingdom, John-Roger

The Emotion Code, Bradley Nelson

Bruce recommends MSIA.org

The best solution is always loving
If you get stuck, give me a call.

6924658R00153

Printed in Great Britain
by Amazon.co.uk, Ltd.,
Marston Gate.